a WORLD of Stone

The Aran islands from earliest times

This book is an account of a people and their place. It opens with a survey of the landscape and environment — the geology, climate, soil and vegetation. It examines the earliest signs of human habitation — the famous dúns of Aran, and gives a detailed account of the most well-known, Dún Aengus.

Next it brings us to the Christian period, when monks and nuns sought isolation in the western islands, and it describes the monasteries and churches to be found on Aran, and tells their history. Then to the Norman period, and to the tragic and difficult Cromwellian experience.

Finally, it deals with the eighteenth and nineteenth centuries when the population on the islands increased — these were centuries of hunger, disease, eviction and emigration.

The focus throughout is on the relationship between the people and the land. The book includes a list of Aran placenames with explanations.

'an unusually rich overview of the land
and its inhabitants'
Choice

First published 1977 by O'Brien Educational
20 Victoria Road, Dublin 6.
Reprinted 1980, 1982, 1985, 1988.

ISBN 0 905140 12 5

10   9   8   7   6   5

Book Design Michael O'Brien
Typesetting Redsetter Limited
Printing I.E.P. Ltd.

"a world of stone"

The Curriculum Development Unit was established in 1972. It is funded by the
City of Dublin Vocational Education Committee. It is managed jointly by the
City of Dublin Vocational Education Committee, Trinity College, Dublin, and
the Department of Education. This book forms part of the Humanities
Curriculum.

Unit Director:	Anton Trant	
Deputy Director:	Tony Crooks	
Humanities Team:		
Tony Crooks	Coordinator 1972-79	
Nora Godwin	1973-79	
	Coordinator 1979-	
Agnes McMahon	1975-76	
Bernard O'Flaherty	1976-78	
Dermot Stokes	1977-82	
Ann Treacy	1978-80	
Patricia McCarthy	1984-	

This collection has been researched and edited by Paul O'Sullivan
with revisions by Nora Godwin.

Prior to publication, the following schools were involved in the development,
use and revision of the collection. The suggestions and comments of the
teachers in these schools have been used as a basis for the edition.
Colaiste Dhulaigh, Coolock; Colaiste Eanna, Cabra; Colaiste Eoin, Finglas;
Coolmine Community School, Clonsilla; Gonzaga College, Dublin; Liberties·
Vocational School, Dublin; Scoil Ide, Finglas; Vocational School, Ballyfermot;
Vocational School for Boys, Clogher Road; Vocational School, Crumlin Road.

*Previous page – The Aran villages occupy sheltered sites on the
broad terraces north of the summit of each island. In the background is the gentle slope of a poorly developed limestone scarp.
The cluster of buildings pre-dated the roads. The small stone walled
fields are hemmed in by areas of bare limestone pavement.*

contents

THE EVENING LAND

From Connemara, or the Moher clifftop,
Where the land ends with a sheer drop,
You can see three stepping stones out of Europe.

Anchored like hulls at the dim horizon
Against the winds' and the waves' explosion.

The Aran Islands are all awash.
East coastline's furled in the foam's white sash.
The clouds melt over them like slush.

And on Galway Bay, between shore and shore,
The ferry plunges to Aranmore.

Seamus Heaney

Limestone pavement on Inishmore criss-crossed by fissures due to the dissolving action of rain water. Much of the surface of all three islands consists of these barren pavements.

ɑRɑՈ ՃíSCOUeReՃ

HE ARAN ISLANDS are a group of windswept grey rock ledges on the Atlantic coast of Ireland. The three main islands are long and low, resembling a group of stranded whales, and together they extend over 25 kilometres in an almost perfectly straight line across the mouth of Galway Bay. The name Aran may have been derived from the Irish word *Ara,* which means a kidney, because of the kidney-like shape of Inishmore. It may equally well have been abbreviated from the Irish expression *Ard-Thuinn,* meaning 'the height above the waves'.

According to legend the islands are the remnants of a rock barrier that once stretched from Galway to Clare, trapping the waters of the present Galway Bay in a gigantic lake. This story has, of course, no basis in fact, but it is worth noting that all three islands are closely related to one another and to the nearby Burren district on the North Clare mainland, in the type and bedding of their rock. The largest of the Aran islands, Inishmore (*Inis Mór* meaning 'the big island') lies nearest to the Galway mainland from which it is separated by the North Sound which is ten kilometres wide. Although this island measures fourteen kilometres by three kilometres at its extremities its total area amounts to little more than thirty one square kilometres. Killeany Bay forms a natural 'waist' to the island lying, as it does within a kilometre of the western cliffs. From there the island rises north westward and achieves its greatest width before descending to the narrow 'neck' at Port Murvey less than a kilometre wide. A second, slightly lower

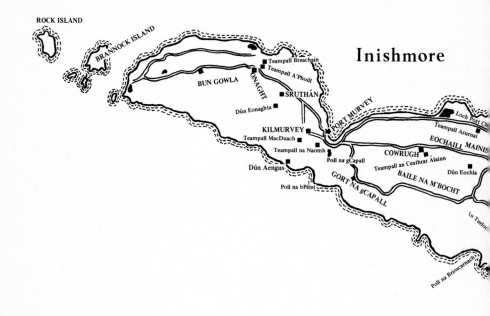

ROCK ISLAND

BRANNOCK ISLAND

Inishmore

Teampall Breachain

Teampall A'Phoill

BUN GOWLA

ONAGHT

SRUTHÁN

Dún Eonaghta

PORT MURVEY

Loch Port Ch

Teampall Asurnai

KILMURVEY

EOCHAILL MAINIS

Teampall MacDuach

COWRUGH

Teampall na Naomh

Teampall an Ceathrar Álainn

Dún Eochla

Poll na gCapall

Dún Aengus

GORT NA gCAPALL

BAILE NA M'BOCHT

Poll na bPéist

In Turloc

Poll na Brioscarnach

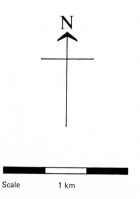

N

Scale   1 km

THE ARAN ISLANDS
County Galway

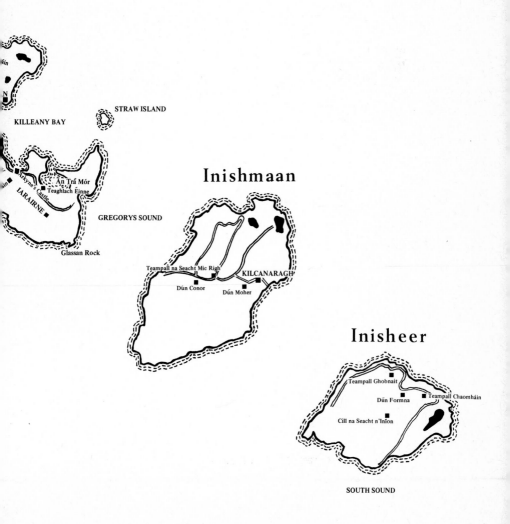

STRAW ISLAND

KILLEANY BAY

Arkyne's Castle

An Trá Mór
Teaghlach Éinne

IARAIRNE

GREGORYS SOUND

Glassan Rock

Inishmaan

Teampall na Seacht Mic Rígh

KILCANARAGH

Dún Conor
Dún Moher

Inisheer

Teampall Ghobnait
Dún Formna
Teampall Chaomháin
Cill na Seacht n'Iníon

SOUTH SOUND

The Atlantic breaks over the rocks at Inishmore.

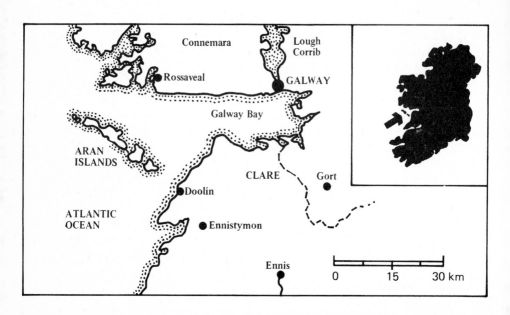

ridge rises to the west of this bay widening the island once more before it slopes gently to the Atlantic at its north-western tip. Inishmaan (*Inis Meáin* — the middle island), lies to the south east of Inishmore across two kilometres of open sea known as Gregory's Sound. It is much smaller than Inishmore, and is more compact in its shape, extending five kilometres from east to west. Inisheer (*Inis Oírr* — the eastern island) is even smaller being an almost regular square with a total area of ten square kilometres. The broad sweep of the South Sound isolates Inisheer from the mainland of Co. Clare, ten kilometres away. A number of small islands complete the Aran group. Rock Island, at the north western tip of Inishmore, is, as the name suggests, a bare rocky surface, inhabited only by the staff who tend the lighthouse erected there in the middle of the nineteenth century. The nearby Brannock Island (*Oileán dá Bhranóg* — the island of the two small ravens) is uninhabited, its limited pastures being grazed by a herd of donkeys. The sandy soils of Straw Island, at the mouth of Killeany Bay, were once utilised to grow rye. It too is uninhabited though an automated lighthouse stands at its western point, a beacon to guide shipping to the piers at Kilronan and Killeany.

Isolation is part of life on Aran. In good weather conditions there is a considerable traffic with the mainland but gale-force winds frequently sever the shipping links and prevent contact with the outside world for weeks on end. The shelving sea bed around the islands makes for a particularly treacherous sea during a storm. The waves break more than a kilometre from the shore, sending gigantic white combers rushing towards the rocks. Life is at its grimmest on the islands when they are stormbound. Communications are cut off, mail and visitors fail to arrive and supplies of food frequently run low. The community is obliged to rely on its own resources to provide for essential needs. Illness during storm conditions is a terrifying prospect. Often a crossing must be attempted, regardless of wind or wave, when a patient is in need of hospitalisation. The islanders grimly joke that a patient in his terror forgets about his illness until he reaches the safety of Rossaveal on the mainland — where his condition immediately deteriorates once more.

For the summer visitor the journey to Aran is a much more pleasant affair. A three hour cruise from Galway city across calm seas brings him within sight of the islands. As the boat approaches its destination, the twin humps of Inishmore, often blurred by mist or haze, assume a more distinct outline. The grey uniformity of the surface rock is the dominant visual tone and only gradually does the observer pick out the golden sandy beaches flecked with the white froth of the breaking waves.

A little higher on the slopes the white and grey washed houses take shape, straggling in an irregular line along the lee side of the ridge. The boat rounds the point of Straw Island and the harbour is now visible, fishing craft in their berths or at anchor, the black crescents of upturned curraghs near the beach, and the confusion of men, animals and goods on the pier head. In the nineteenth century the journey had to be made by curragh, a colourful and exciting experience for the stranger.

RACING WITH THE WAVES

J. M. Synge visited the Aran Islands each summer during the years 1898 to 1902, and he lived with families on Inishmore and Inishmaan. His book, *The Aran Islands,* is an account of life on the islands at that time. In this excerpt, Synge describes a curragh ride in rough seas on his way to the islands.

WE SET OFF. IT WAS A four-oared curragh, and I was given the last seat so as to leave the stern for the man who was steering with an oar, worked at right angles to the others by an extra thole-pin in the stern gunnel.

When we had gone about a hundred yards they ran up a bit of a sail in the bow and the pace became extraordinarily rapid.

The shower had passed over and the wind had fallen, but large, magnificently brilliant waves were rolling down on us at right angles to our course.

Every instant the steersman whirled us round with a sudden stroke of his oar, the prow reared up and then fell into the next furrow with a crash, throwing up masses of spray. As it did so, the stern in its turn was thrown up, and both the steersman, who let go his oar and clung with both hands to the gunnel, and myself, were lifted high up above the sea.

The wave passed, we regained our course and rowed violently for a few yards, when the same manoeuvre had to be repeated. As we worked out into the sound we began to meet another class of waves, that could be seen for some distance towering above the rest.

When one of these came in sight, the first effort was to get beyond its reach. The steersman began crying out in Gaelic

'Siubhal, siubhal' ('Run, run'), and sometimes, when the mass was gliding towards us with horrible speed, his voice rose to a shriek. Then the rowers themselves took up the cry, and the curragh seemed to leap and quiver with the frantic terror of a beast till the wave passed behind it or fell with a crash beside the stern.

It was in this racing with the waves that our chief danger lay. If the wave could be avoided, it was better to do so, but if it overtook us while we were trying to escape, and caught us on the broadside, our destruction was certain. I could see the steersman quivering with the excitement of his task, for any error in his judgment would have swamped us.

We had one narrow escape. A wave appeared high above the rest, and there was the usual moment of intense exertion. It was of no use, and in an instant the wave seemed to be hurling itself upon us. With a yell of rage the steersman struggled with his oar to bring our prow to meet it. He had almost succeeded, when there was a crash and rush of water round us. I felt as if I had been struck upon the back with knotted ropes. White foam gurgled round my knees and eyes. The curragh reared up, swaying and trembling for a moment, and then fell safely into the furrow.

This was our worst moment, though more than once, when several waves came so closely together that we had no time to regain control of the canoe between them, we had some dangerous work. Our lives depended upon the skill and courage of the men, as the life of the rider or swimmer is often in his own hands, and the excitement of the struggle was too great to allow time for fear.

I enjoyed the passage. Down in this shallow trough of canvas that bent and trembled with the motion of the men, I had a far more intimate feeling of the glory and power of the waves than I have ever known in a steamer.

the physical landscape

HOUGH INISHMAAN AND Inisheer differ from Inishmore in their size and shape and orientation, the three islands possess similar landscapes with each island duplicating on a lesser scale the slope outline of its larger neighbour. Each slopes gently to the waters of Galway Bay on its north east face. They rise inland in a series of terraces before dipping once more to meet the Atlantic waves on their south west sides.

Inishmore shows the characteristic Aran landscape in its most extreme form. A series of eight distinct terraces, each with a well developed scarp or cliff, rises inland like a giant's staircase on each of the two hill masses which make up the greater part of the island's surface. These 'steps' rise to an altitude of 124 metres at Oghil, the highest point in the whole of the Aran group, and they attain an altitude of 108 metres in a parallel sequence on the western hill at Onaght. From these central heights the land dips gently westward to the coast before plunging abruptly over sheer cliffs to the Atlantic waves below. The visually impressive scarps which front the steps, are minor limestone cliffs ranging from three to five metres in height. The scarps are most sheer and the terraces narrowest near the north-east shore. Inland, the terraces are much wider, the most extensive pair being each one kilometre wide in parts. These latter terraces are well sheltered and are the sites for all but one of the islands fourteen 'villages'. In the low neck of the island at Port Murvey a single terrace offers a site to Gort na gCapall, the only village on the western or Atlantic side of the island.

Inishmaan and Inisheer display a similar sequence of steps but their cliffs are much lower and less continuous than those in Inishmore.

Within each of the islands, there are three distinct types of landscape. Each has extensive areas of low lying sand dunes on the north shore, the sand giving way to shingle and gravel on Inishmore. Inland the slope rises in a series of terraces which have been favoured sites for settlement and agriculture. Finally, south west of the summits, there are areas of sparsely vegetated rock known in each case as "the back of the island" and utilised, only in a limited way, as winter grazing.

The most visually impressive landscape feature in the Aran group, the feature which binds all three islands into a geographical and geological unity, is the expanse of bare limestone pavement found on each.

The limestones of Ireland were formed 350 million years ago when much of the country was submerged under a warm, shallow sea. This sea teemed with marine life forms whose calcium rich bones and shells fell to the sea bed when they died. The pressure of the sea water combined with natural cementing agents to bond these layers of shells and bones into the rock we know as limestone.

Limestone is classified as a sedimentary rock by geologists, which means that it is formed from particles of material, or sediments, which settled, or came to rest, at the bottom of the sea. The Aran limestones contain many fossils, the preserved remains of some of the marine organisms which went to make up the rock. Within the limestone we can easily identify layers or strata and the bedding planes which separate them. The Aran beds are tilted gently to the south west. In fact this 'dip' slope of the rock corresponds with the gentle slope from the summit to the cliffs at the "back of the island".

In the Aran islands, and in the similar Burren area of North Clare the massive blocks of limestone are exposed at the surface and are almost completely devoid of any soil cover. This type of bare limestone landscape is known as Karst, taking its name from the Karst area of Yugoslavia where geologists first studied it.

It seemed possible that the Aran islands did not always have a barren limestone surface. The ice sheets which melted at the end of the Ice Age 10,000 years ago probably left a blanket of boulder clay (a mixture of crushed rock, sand and gravel) over most of the islands. Bad farming practices combined with the power of the wind and the rain have resulted in the erosion of this covering and in the exposure of the limestone beneath.

The chemicals contained in limestone are easily dissolved by rain water which sometimes contains a weak carbonic acid. The rainwater attacks exposed limestone along joints and cracks and lines of weakness enlarging them into wide, deep fissures. Annual rainfall totals are high in the islands but the water quickly percolates down through the fissures and the landscape presents an arid face, weathered to a remarkable crazy pavement effect.

The massive grey limestones of Aran are interbedded with thin bands of shale, a rock which has a much greater resistance to the erosive action of rainwater. This difference in the rates of erosion of the two rocks creates the stepped landscape which is character-istic of Inishmore in particular.

The absence of surface water is the most striking feature of the drainage pattern on the islands. Rainfall disappears through the fissures almost as soon as it has fallen and surface streams frequently dry up altogether in summer. An example of such an intermittent stream is found at Sruthán on Inishmore.

Although water can pass freely through limestone it is unable to penetrate the shale beds beneath and its downward movement is halted. It then collects at the bedding plane which separates the limestone from the shale and flows along the dip slope of the rock as an underground stream. Such streams eventually emerge on the slopes at the base of the limestone scarps where they provide a water supply for the villages.

Droughts frequently occur during the summer months when rain may not fall for several weeks at a time. Surface streams dry up completely and the islanders have difficulty in finding sufficient water to supply the animals in their fields. Since the 1920's the Inishmore farmers, aided by Government grants, have constructed numerous rain troughs in their fields. These troughs are fashioned from slabs of limestone pointed with cement and each has a surface area of about six square metres. In order to increase the catchment potential of these troughs an apron, or platform, is built onto one or more sides of the trough. This apron, six to nine square metres in area, slopes at an angle of about thirty degrees to the lip of the trough allowing any water which lands on its surface to drain into the trough. The surface of the apron is cemented over in order to prevent the precious rain water from seeping down through the limestone blocks of which it is built. On the smaller islands there is less need for these rain troughs as each individual's house is located much nearer to his fields and there is less labour involved in carrying water to the grazing animals.

An interesting feature of drainage on Aran are the turloughs which are found at An Turloch Mór and Poll na gCapall on Inishmore. A turlough (*tur loch* — a dry lake) is an impermanent lake which occurs in a shallow depression in the limestone. When heavy rainfall occurs the level of permanent water saturation in the ground, known as the water table, rises rapidly and the turlough fills up, often in a matter of hours. During a period of exceptionally heavy rainfall the turlough may flood surrounding fields. In a dry summer, however, the water table will drop allowing the water of the lake to drain through fissures in the lake bed. The turlough will shrink to pond size, or it may, in a prolonged drought, dry up completely, providing good temporary grazing for cattle and sheep.

THE WORK OF THE SEA

The south-west face of each of the Aran islands lies open to the great Atlantic breakers which are driven shorewards by the prevailing south-west winds. Mountainous waves batter the islands in Autumn and Winter, waves which have travelled across the wide Atlantic and which are meeting with resistance for the first time. The erosive power of these waves is great even in calm weather. In storm conditions they exert a tremendous pressure on the cliffs, hurling boulders and rock fragments against them, and occasionally tossing huge rocks right over the cliff top.

Inishmore is edged on its west side with a continuous line of remarkably sheer cliffs. The coastlines of Inishmaan and Inisheer are lower, but where cliffs occur on these islands they also tend to be sheer. The clean vertical face of the cliffs, free of any rock outcrops, allows the islanders to fish from the top with a heavily weighted line. This practice of cliff-top fishing for wrasse, known locally as rockfish, was common in the past. In the mid-nineteenth century a tragedy occurred at Glassan Rock, near the south eastern end of Inishmore, which is still recalled in the island today. Fifteen men from Killeany village who were fishing from a ledge were swept into the sea by a freak wave and were drowned.

Above — The shifting sand dunes of Inisheer are believed to have buried a number of ancient settlements. Teampall Chaomhair has escaped the same fate only because the sand is shovelled out of the building each year on June 14th, the saint's feast day.

Left — Limestone pavement eroding under the influence of the sea spray. Rock pools formed in this way are common on Inishmore.

Almost every household in the little village was bereaved of a husband or son in the disaster, which, according to popular lore, was occasioned by the fact that the men had not attended mass on the day in question which was a church Holy Day.

Other features of note on the highland coast of Inishmore are the sea arch at Poll na Brioscarnach and the strange natural 'swimming pool' at Poll na bPéist. This latter feature is a rectangular basin in the rock, into which the sea flows through a submarine passage, the legendary haunt of a sea monster. When, in a storm, water swells through the access passage, it shoots a jet into the air not unlike the spouting of a monster. Poll na bPéist is just one of a number of such puffing holes found on Inishmore and Inishmaan.

All three islands have storm beaches on their southern and south western shores. The storm beaches are lines of massive boulders which have been tossed over the cliff top in severe storms, coming to rest in a jumbled line — a visible testament to the power of the angry sea.

The more sheltered north-east shores of the islands present a contrasting face. The three islands slope, or step, gently down to Galway Bay and the sea bed shelves gradually towards the Connemara mainland. Even up to three kilometres north of Inishmore depths of less than ten fathoms can be recorded. This lowland coast has been shaped by marine deposition rather than by erosion. Extensive beaches of shingle and sand have been laid down here and the north east corner of each island is a landscape of shifting sand dunes. The roof of the ancient church, Teaghlach Éinne, near Iarairne is on the same level as the top of the dunes which surround it and the church of St. Cavan of Inisheer has to be regularly cleared of sand drifts. The dunes are devoid of houses, roads and fences and are held as commonage by groups of island families. An Trá Mór, the magnificent stretch of beach at the eastern end of Inishmore, is a lagoon in the making as it is gradually being cut off from the open sea by sandpits. Loch Port Charruch and Loch Dearg, on the same island, are lagoons which were cut off from the sea by shingle bars.

CLIMATE

The hallmark of the daily weather on the islands, as elsewhere in Ireland, is its changeability. The sky may cloud up or clear to a radiant blue within a matter of hours and a rainy day is often interrupted by a few hours of sunshine when the glistening rock pavements create the illusion of a landscape of shallow lakes. As one local man observed, "the four seasons all come in one day".

The climate of Aran, like that of Ireland generally is oceanic and it is characteristically mild, moist and equable. The influence of the ocean is important, as summer temperatures seldom exceed 16°C due to the cool breezes. Similarly, winter temperatures seldom drop below 5°C and frost and snow are a rarity. Low annual and daily temperature ranges are typical of the islands' climate. The North Atlantic Drift, a warm ocean current which originates in the Gulf of Mexico, flows along the west coast of Ireland and is particularly effective in keeping winter temperatures well above freezing point.

The pattern of rainfall on Aran is broadly similar to that found throughout the western part of Ireland. Ireland lies in the direct path of the south-west winds, winds which are laden with moisture because they have passed over a relatively warm ocean where constant evaporation goes on. West coast locations received the brunt of this rainfall and the Aran islands have a high annual total of rainfall relative to places in the centre of the country or on the east coast. The mountainous Galway mainland, being higher, has an even greater annual rainfall than the Aran group, the highest point of which stands only 124 metres above sea level.

This table gives the monthly average rainfall (mm.) and temperatures (degrees Celsius) for the Aran Islands.

Jan.	Feb.	Mar.	Apr.	May	June	July	Aug.	Sept.	Oct.	Nov.	Dec.
116	79	73	62	65	73	83	105	119	126	115	136
5.8	6.0	7.7	9.0	11.3	14.0	15.2	15.3	13.8	11.0	8.4	6.8

Rainfall is well distributed throughout the year — even the driest month, April, has a substantial amount — but the nature of the surface rock exaggerates the effects of even a short drought and dry sunny summers result in rapid evaporation from the shallow soils.

Most typical of late autumn, winter and spring is a misty foggy type of weather when a fine drizzle falls for hours on end. Such a day, mild but very wetting, is described as a "lá bog" or a soft day. Fogs frequently hang about the shores of Galway Bay proving hazardous to sailor and fisherman alike. Stories are told of currach crews being enveloped in dense fog and losing their way, rowing until they dropped from exhaustion.

The first lighthouse to be erected on Aran was built in the early

19th century at the highest point of Inishmore near Dún Eochla. This lighthouse is a prominent feature of the Inishmore skyline from almost any vantage point on the island. It was, however, too high to be of any use as a beacon in foggy conditions and even in clear conditions ships lying in close to the cliffs on the south side could not see the light which might have warned them of their danger. This lighthouse was soon replaced by the structure on Rock Island. A similar lighthouse was erected at Pointe an Fhardarus, the south east tip of Inisheer, to mark the other extremity of the islands.

On a clear day the view from the cliffs of Inishmore or Inishmaan is unsurpassable. The absence of pollution and the constant sea breezes give a remarkable clarity to the air and it is easy to pick out the long sloping shoreline of Co. Clare, and, far to the south, the promontory of Kerry Head on the other side of the Shannon. It may also be possible to see, in the right meteorological conditions, the celebrated mirage known variously as Hy Brasil or Tír na nÓg. This illusion has been frequently observed, lying between the Irish Coast and the horizon, and folklore has represented it as being, among other things, the Garden of Eden, the land of eternal youth and a lost Atlantis-like continent.

The Aran islands are low-lying and they seem to crouch before the winds which whip across them in winter. Gales are a frequent occurrence and the south westerlies are often accompanied by mountainous seas. Winds registering Force 10 and Force 11 on the Beaufort scale often buffet the islands in autumn and winter. Some of the worst gales on record have come in late September and early October. The absence of settlement on the south and west side of the ridges on all three islands becomes understandable when one has experienced a storm in Aran. As long ago as 1684 Roderick O'Flaherty recorded in his *Chorographical Description of West Connacht* that a gigantic wave swept across the low neck of Inishmore between Gort na gCapall and Kilmurvey in 1640 A.D. Independent evidence records the occurrence of an earthquake on the north-west coasts of Europe at about that time. It seems possible that the wave which O'Flaherty noted in his history was a tidal wave associated with these earth tremors.

SOILS

It is thought that the islands may once have had an adequate soil cover though today they present a largely barren rock surface.

Such soils, if they did exist were probably formed on a parent material of boulder clay which the retreating ice sheets left behind 100,000 years ago.

The soils now found on the islands are the result of the weathering of exposed shale beds. Natural soils have been unable to develop on the limestone pavement because water dissolves rather than breaks up the rock. The layer of rock fragments and powder which has developed on the shale and which bacteria and other organisms change into soil, has never formed on the limestone.

ERRATICS

Great round boulders of granite are found scattered about the pavement at the eastern and western ends of Inishmore. The crystalline nature of these rocks contrasts strongly with the uniform grey of the limestone on which they rest. Folktales explain them as the missiles of an angry giant who lived in Connemara, an explanation not too far removed from the scientific facts. They are, in fact, glacial erratics, huge boulders which were moved from their place of origin by the advancing ice sheets and dumped unceremoniously when the temperatures rose once again and a thaw set in. These erratics have been incorporated into the stone walls of the island and some were shaped into Bullauns — rocks hollowed into a basin which may have been used as a bowl in which to grind corn by the early Christian monks or by pre-Christian farmers.

VEGETATION

We will never know what kind of natural vegetation might have evolved on the Aran islands had man never set foot on them. Man has destroyed soil and made soil; he has fertilised the land and exhausted the land; he has tilled fields and built walls and broken the flat surface of the pavements. His activities have had an influence on the various habitats available to plants. Other factors such as the nature of the rock, the distribution, depth and type of the soil, the relief and slope of the land, the amount and distribution of rainfall and the daily and yearly temperature patterns have all influenced the evolution of the local vegetation.

Four distinct habitats can be identified. On the limestone pavements, soil can be found only in the fissures or grykes which crisscross the landscape. This habitat offers limited soil and light and there is an absence of permanent water at root level though rainwater regularly passes through the fissures. A variety of ferns thrive on this habitat, particularly the Maiden Hair Fern and the Hart's Tongue Fern. Flowering plants which can tolerate the alkaline salts in the pockets of soil are common, and rare species such as Alpine Spring Gentian can also be found. The fissures also support a number of varieties of dwarfed trees, including hazel, hawthorn and blackthorn which enjoy a stunted growth up to ground level.

In many places the pavement environment has been modified by man's creation of soil. This distinctive habitat displays the ordinary range of meadow grasses and flowers as well as some rarer lime-tolerant plants. On many of the scarp faces a growth of ivy is found and it also thrives on the ruined walls of dwelling houses. At the base of some scarps, where springs issue from the rock, hydrophytes are common.

Thirdly, the sand-dunes provide a severely limited environment for some varieties of sedges and grasses. The shifting sands are suitable only to plants with a brief life-cycle whose processes of growth and reproduction can be accomplished in the shortest space of time. Water drains quickly through the porous sands and the wind regularly whips up sand storms. For these reasons the dune plants must develop deep root systems, or a network of

The surface of the limestone pavement offers neither soil nor shelter nor moisture for plant growth. Only in the fissures and crevasses has soil accumulated and is there shelter to be found from the wind.

The remains of a dolmen on Inishmaan. This tomb is one of the indications that the islands were inhabited in the Megalithic period.

roots which extend laterally, serving to anchor the plant as well as to seek out moisture. Man-made walls provide some shelter and allow plants to establish themselves.

The shore between High Water Mark and Low Water Mark is a fourth habitat. Algaes of the usual varieties are found some of which, such as kelp and bladder-wrack, are of economic importance. These seaweeds grow better on the north and east shores than they do on the more exposed western shores.

The absence of large trees on all three islands is visually one of the most striking features. Folklore and local placenames would seem to indicate that the islands were once wooded. The place name Eochla, for instance, is thought to refer to a stand of yew trees. It is unlikely though that anything other than shrubs or scrubby woodland ever grew on the islands due to a general lack of shelter from the prevailing south westerly winds. The few trees and bushes one meets with on the bend of the main road west of Cowrugh on Inishmore, are stunted in their growth and, in their branch formation, lean heavily away from the wind. Inishmaan has a single tree, Inisheer has none at all. The only stand of trees in the whole island group are those which were planted in the grounds of the rectory at Kilronan in the late 19th century.

the Dúns
of aran

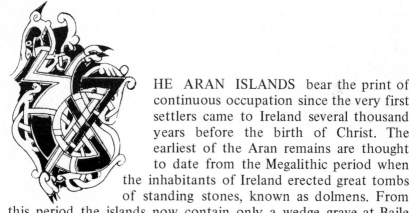

HE ARAN ISLANDS bear the print of
continuous occupation since the very first
settlers came to Ireland several thousand
years before the birth of Christ. The
earliest of the Aran remains are thought
to date from the Megalithic period when
the inhabitants of Ireland erected great tombs
of standing stones, known as dolmens. From
this period the islands now contain only a wedge grave at Baile
Sean on Inishmore, a ruined dolmen on Inishmaan, some lesser
remains on Inisheer and a Megalithic settlement buried beneath
the shifting sands of Iarairne. This settlement lay exposed and
was studied around the middle of the 19th century. The great
stone forts are undoubtedly the most impressive of the remains
found on the islands today. As one approaches Inishmore the
primitive outline of Dún Eochla appears on the skyline. Further
west is the barbaric magnificence of the Dún Aengus site and Dún
Conor dominates from its hilltop position, the whole landscape of
Inishmaan. They are massive structures of dry-stone masonry,
a building technique widely employed in the Celtic period,
perhaps even in the pre-Celtic period. The technology of these
early builders did not include the use of mortar, that is any filling
or binding agent such as mud or cement. Mortared buildings came
into Ireland only with the advent of the Normans in the late 12th
century. Mortared structures such as the castle begin to assume a
place in the landscape from that date onwards. The dry-stone of
the fort building however, is still used by the ordinary Aran farmer
in breaking down and building up some of the 11,000 kilometres

of stone walls which divide up his island into a patchwork of tiny fields.

The fort builders used the material which was all around them, that is, limestone, a rock that is very easily split and shaped. Like all Aran men they knew how to make best use of the local rock and their structures were carefully built to withstand weathering and time. Stones are massive at the base of the walls and they rise layer upon layer, bracing one another, through careful selection and skilful placing. The wall of each fort was constructed by first of all building up two walls with a space between them and filling in this space with limestone rubble and smaller rocks. Each wall is terraced so that while it is six metres wide at the base it narrows to about two metres wide at the top. Within some of the forts are the jumbled ruins of dwelling houses, stone buildings of dry stone construction. Some also contain souterrains, underground passages leading to a point outside the walls. These may have been used for the storage of food or as an exit route in an emergency.

Though the origins of the forts are clouded in mystery, scholars now agree that they may not be as ancient as was first thought. They may have existed as early as the 8th century B.C. but it seems more likely that they were built in the 1st or 2nd century B.C. and that they were used throughout the early Christian period and even into the Middle Ages. Similar stone forts were being constructed elsewhere in the country as late as the year 1100 A.D. and evidence from Co. Clare suggests that they were in daily use even in the 16th century.

Island folklore claims that the forts were built by the Fir Bolg, a prehistoric tribe who invaded the country but were defeated by subsequent invaders. The Fir Bolg then fled from the mainland and sought refuge on Aran and other west-coast islands. The legends say that they built the forts as a defensive measure as they prepared to make their last stand. Those who put forward this claim point to the massiveness of the stone walls, to the sites being on or near hilltops and to the barrenness of the Aran landscape as proof. Why should they have come here unless they had been forced to, such scholars say. They forget, however, that the Ireland of even one thousand years ago was a country of woodland, bog and swamp where communication was difficult and dangerous. Coastal locations were regarded as prime sites. The land of Aran was probably not always as barren as it is today and the islands were not merely a wasteland with no possible use other

◀*The massive wall of Dún Dú-chathair seen from inside the fortification. The rough dry stone wall rises by means of two ramparts to a total height of 6 metres. In the foreground can be seen the ruins of the clochans or stone huts which were the probable dwellings of the original inhabitants of the duns.*

Below — The chevaux-de-frise of Dun Aengus. This remarkable barrier of razor-sharp standing stones was certainly a defensive measure. A small band of defenders could, from the safety of the third wall, in the background, inflict heavy losses on enemies who were attempting to pick their way through this solid 'barbed wire'.

than for defensive purposes. The tradition which associates Dun Aengus with the Firbolg Prince Aengus may be no more than a few centuries old. But most important of all is the fact that none of the Dun sites contain a source of fresh water and so these structures can hardly have been intended as refuges which could hold out against a long siege. The building of the Duns must have required a huge expenditure of time, manpower and materials, and can hardly have been the work of a defeated people making a last ditch stand on an Atlantic cliff-top. It is much more likely that they are the proud monuments of a prosperous and aggressive people. Their owners were probably rich farmers, as all of the forts are situated close to some of the best agricultural land on their respective islands. Early writers, such as Roderick O'Flaherty in the 17th century, described the forts in terms of the number of cattle which they might have held, a probable clue to their original use.

Thirty to forty thousand forts were scattered throughout Ireland in the pre-Norman period. They were the dwellings of the 'strong' farmers in each district. In fertile parts of the country the fort, known as a Lios or a Rath, was made up of one or more earthen banks. In the western part of the country the fort was known as a dun or cathair or caiseal and was built of stone. Stone was readily available and it is an easily used material and the building of the walls helped in the clearing of the land. There were probably other cathairs and duns on the Aran Islands which were not as sturdily built or not as well preserved as those that survived. The remains of stone walls at Baile na Sean and Baile na mBocht on Inishmore may have once been part of the walls of a number of Duns. These, and other forts, crumbled or were dismantled to provide building stone for houses or walls. The Aran duns are all large and strongly built and it has been suggested that they were the homes of clan groups rather than of individual families. Then, as now, an individual or group with a surplus of wealth tended to convert it into a prestigious monument usually in a prominent site.

There was, however, some consideration of defence present in the minds of the dun builders. The sites, on hill tops and cliff tops, the strength of the walls and the presence around some forts of *chevaux de frise,* or lines of strategically placed standing stones, would seem to indicate a definite defensive intent. The lack of fresh water meant that they were unsuitable for a prolonged siege so they were probably used as a refuge during the short-lived attacks by pirates or mainland raiders.

The Aran forts are of two kinds, Dún Conor and Dún Eochla are examples of hill forts, and Dún Eonaghta, while not at the highest point of its hill, is located very near the summit. Dún Dúchathair is a perfect example of a promontory fort, that is, a fort built on a headland which needs only a single wall as it has the cliffs for protection on three sides. Dún Aengus has elements of both the hill-top and promontory types. In all, there are remains of seven forts on the islands, four on Inishmore, two on Inishmaan and one on Inisheer. It should be remembered however, that almost all of the forts were repaired by the Board of Works in the 1890's, using the best knowledge and craftsmanship available at that time. The buttresses which bolster up the inner wall of Dún Aengus were built at that time and the regular outline of the walls of all of the forts is probably a false picture of what they originally looked like.

DÚN AENGUS

Dún Aengus is the most impressive, and the most famous, of all the Aran forts. It is a spectacular structure, both in the enormous scale of its walls and in the precarious cliff top site it occupies. It consists of four roughly concentric walls, all of which back onto a cliff edge with a sheer drop of several hundred feet to the pounding Atlantic waves below. One may be tempted, on first viewing Dún Aengus, to regard it as the remaining half of an ordinary ringfort, the rest of which has been destroyed by the erosion of the cliff on which it is set. But it is highly unlikely that there ever was "another half". The plan of the fort could hardly be bettered, making use, as it does, of the cliff edge as an absolute protection against attack from the west side.

The innermost of the four enclosures resembles half of an oval with an east-west diameter of forty-two metres. It is surrounded by a wall, four metres wide at the base, which rises up to six metres in two terraces. On the east side a doorway, whose massive lintels still remain in place, afforded entry and exit to the dun-dwellers. In the centre of the enclosure, backing onto the lip of the cliff, is a rectangular platform, twelve metres by nine, which is nothing more than a natural rock outcrop though it has been described as a man-made 'table' or 'altar'.

Outside this enclosure is a second wall which follows the curve of the inner wall before extending eastward to take in a consider-

Dún Aengus from the air, showing the sequence of four walls. The cliff top position, magnificent and precarious, seems to imply a defensive intent by the dún builders. The main enclosure is horse-shoe shaped and was never at any time a circular ring fort as some scholars have claimed. In the centre of the horse-shoe, at the very cliff edge is a remarkable 'table' of rock, a natural outcrop. The sheer nature of the Aran cliffs and the well defined bedding planes of the rock can be clearly seen.

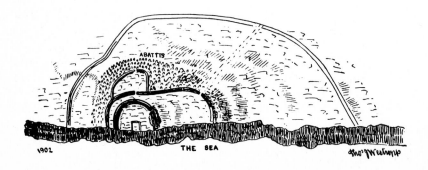

1902   ABATTIS   THE SEA

able area of land before finally meeting the cliff face. Further out are fragments of a third wall which once followed the general outline of the other walls. It is believed that this third wall was demolished in order to provide stone for the building of the fourth wall — a massive structure which extends 400 metres and encloses a D-shaped plot, 4.5 hectares in area.

Between the third and fourth walls are the well preserved remains of a *chevaux de frise*. This is an arrangement of closely spaced standing stones, some up to 1.5 metres in height, which slope toward one another, making a passage through them slow and difficult. John O'Donovan of the Ordnance Survey wrote this description of the *chevaux de frise* at Dún Aengus in 1839: "Some of these stones appear at a distance like soldiers making the onset, and many of them are so sharp that if one fell against them they would run him through. This army of stones would appear to have been intended by the Bolgae of Aran to answer the same purpose as the modern chevaux de Frise, now generally used in making a retrenchment to stop cavalry; but these stones were never intended to keep off horses, as no horses could come near the place without 'breaking their legs'. They must have been, therefore, used for keeping off men, and very well adapted they are for this purpose, for a few men standing on the outer wall just described, could by casting stones, kill hundreds of invaders while attempting to pass through this army of sharp stones."

Even today, after centuries of exposure to the weather, some of these standing stones remain razor sharp to the touch. The *chevaux de frise* probably extended right round the original third wall of the fort but it is preserved only on the north side. One can only wonder as to why the dun dwellers decided to build a fourth wall outside the *chevaux de frise* and to do so tore down the easily defended third wall. The size of the enclosure and the sheer length of the fourth wall would have made it almost impossible to defend so we can only conclude that this last wall was built much later than the others, during a peaceful era when the old fortifications were no longer regarded as essential. If this is so the eleven acres enclosure may have been envisaged as an elaborate cattle pen rather than an additional defensive measure.

The name Dún Aengus has been traditionally associated with the mythical Firbolg prince Aengus and some stories have it that the fort is the resting place of the Firbolg warriors who lie there awaiting the call to arms once more.

OTHER FORTS

Dún Dúchathair (The Black Fort) is situated on a promontory to the east of Dún Aengus. Here the cliffs are much lower, but they surround the fort on three sides affording it excellent protection. The fort itself consists of a single roughly constructed wall, sixty metres in length, which runs across the neck of the promontory providing an effective and easily defended barrier. The wall, like that of Dún Aengus, rises in two steps and a *chevaux de frise* of standing stones on the landward side combine with the sheer cliffs to make this a secure defensive site.

Dún Eochla (the fort of the Yew Wood) is a well preserved example of a hill fort. It is situated near to the highest point of Inishmore commanding a magnificent view of the sea approaches on all sides of the island. Dún Eochla consists of two roughly concentric massively built walls, the inner having a diameter of 23 metres. Within this inner circle is a large mount of loose stone which was built up during reconstruction work in the late nineteenth century. These stones are believed to be the last remnants of the clochans or stone huts which formerly housed the occupants of the dun.

Dún Eonaghta (the fort of the Eonaght tribe) is situated on the western hill of Inishmore near to a summit or altitude of 108 metres. It also is a circular hill fort but consists of one wall only. The name Eonaght is believed to be associated with a Munster tribe who are reputed to have occupied part of the island at one time. Dún Eonaghta is situated within reach of some relatively good agricultural land and overlooks the site which was later chosen for one of the major monasteries of Aran. The fort itself was probably the residence of a farming clan group.

Dún Conor, on Inishmaan, is the largest of all the Aran ring forts, and is the finest example of a hill fort in Ireland. It occupies a splendid site on the north side of the central summit of the island. The enclosed area five thousand five hundred square metres in extent, is surrounded by a wall up to six metres high in parts. As in the other forts, this wall has a wide base, and it rises in two steps so that it is much narrower at the top. An outer wall takes the form of a semi-circle around the north and east sides of the fort. This wall does not extend to the south or west sides of the inner circle as a steep rocky slope on these sides probably convinced the dun builders that the natural defences were already adequate. At the northernmost corner of this outer wall there is a small walled enclosure which may have acted as a defensive gateway. Within the fort are the remains of structures which must have originally been clochans or dry-stone beehive huts.

The land around Dún Conor is among the best available on Inishmaan and many of the island farmers own fields in the vicinity of the fort. From the topmost rampart one can see how the fields with their stone walls follow the lines of the fortification.

In a crevice in the wall of the fort, a mainland man named Malley who had accidentally killed his father in a fit of passion, was hidden by the islanders for several months before he managed to make good his escape to America. This incident, reputed to have occurred sometime during the nineteenth century, was related to J. M. Synge. The playwright was much taken with the story and he later used it as the inspiration for the plot of his famous comedy *The Playboy of the Western World.*

The other ringfort of Inishmaan, Dún Moher, also known as Dún Fhearbhaigh is less impressive than Dún Conor, being a smaller D-shaped structure. It too is situated in good farmland and was also the probable dwelling of a tribal farming group.

The hilltop fort of Dún Formna is situated near to the highest point of Inisheer, a commanding position over the occupied northern part of the island. Only one wall of this fort has survived and though considerable in its extent it is less massive in its construction than that of any of the other forts. Within Dún Formna a castle was constructed in the sixteenth century by the O'Brien clan of Co. Clare, who ruled the Aran Islands at that time. This castle probably utilised the old line of the Dun as an outer defensive barrier. These two buildings, their origins separated by at least one thousand years of history, share the prime site of the island, and the building techniques used in each contrast strongly. The mortared masonry of the castle is a product of the Norman invasion. The dry-stone masonry of the dun wall that surrounds it is more primitive perhaps, but it makes for an equally sturdy fortification.

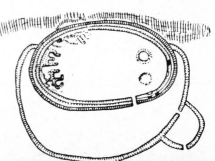

Plan of Dun Conor, Inishmaan.
The enclosed area is 5,500 sq.
metres in extent.

INISHEER

We first drop anchor, beyond the pier,
Off the first island called Inisheer,
Where all the islandmen and women
Wear bright-knit shawls and well-patched homespun,
The women with rainbows round their shoulders,
The oarsmen strong and grey as boulders.
The currachs that lie along the strand
Are hoisted up. Black new moons walk the sand
And down where the waves break in white lace.
The bobbing boats all plunge and race
And row right under the steamer's bows —
Then back they ride with homely cargoes.

Seamus Heaney

ara na naomh

HRISTIANITY FIRST CAME to Ireland in the early part of the fifth century A.D. and it is believed to have been brought to Aran by St. Enda who founded a monastery at Killeany, on Inishmore, in the year 490 A.D. Enda's foundation was one of the earliest and one of the most important monasteries of the period. It became famous throughout Ireland and holy men flocked there to lead a life of study and prayer. Many of those trained in the monastic life of Aran later founded monasteries of their own elsewhere in Ireland or on the continent of Europe. Several of the Fathers of the early Irish Church studied in Aran or visited the islands which were widely known as Ara na Naomh — Aran of the Saints.

A typical monastery would have centred on a group of small churches where the monks could pray privately or in small groups. The monks would have lived in huts or cells nearby, which, in Aran would have taken the form of beehive huts called clochans, built of dry-stone masonry. The monastery would also contain workshops for blacksmiths and scribes and, perhaps, a building to house visitors and travellers. The whole monastic settlement would have been surrounded by an earthen bank or stone wall. The monastic site would usually have been marked by stone crosses. At first these crosses were cut into the face of any convenient boulder but later the stone was shaped into the form of a cross. As the skill of the stone-cutters developed over the centuries they began to decorate the crosses with elaborate designs and lettering. Many magnificent examples of these High Crosses can still be seen throughout Ireland.

The monks lived under a strict rule devoting their lives to work and prayer. At set times during the day and night they gathered in the churches to pray. On Wednesdays and Fridays they fasted taking only one meal each day at evening time. Lent was observed as a time of special fasting and penance.

The monastery farm provided for all the needs of the community. The monks grew corn which they milled by hand to make bread. They kept herds of cattle and sheep, and in some cases, chickens and bees. Where possible fish from the lakes and sea was part of their diet.

Many of the monasteries had schools attached which attracted students from Britain and Europe. Some of the monks worked as scribes copying the gospels by hand onto sheets of cured cowhide called vellum. Annals, accounts of the important events which occurred in the locality each year, were also compiled. Manuscripts of this kind were almost certainly compiled on Aran but none has survived. However many beautifully coloured and intricately lettered books from monasteries elsewhere in Ireland are preserved in museums and libraries.

Monastic life flourished in Ireland, and in Aran, during the centuries following Enda's death, a period often referred to as The Golden Age. Aran contains the remains of two major monastic settlements, one situated at Killeany on Inishmore, the other at Onaght, further west on the same island. Numerous other remains are found in between these sites and on Inishmaan and Inisheer.

KILLEANY

Enda, the patron saint of Aran, is believed to have been born in Leinster and to have been converted to a Christian vocation through the efforts of his sister who was a nun. After founding a small monastery in the Boyne Valley he lived in Scotland for a number of years before returning to establish foundations in other parts of Ireland. Finally he came to Aran, the place most closely associated with his name. According to legend he was miraculously transported over the waves in a stone boat coming to land near Killeany where he set about building one of the great influential monasteries of the age. The name Cill Éinne (Killeany) means, literally, The Church of Enda.

The remains of Enda's monastery are situated on the edge of An Trá Mór, the Big Strand, at the eastern end of Inishmore. All

1897   J.J.W.

Portions of a cross shaft which have been cemented together on the site of Enda's monastery. The intricate carving was typical of the high crosses of the period. The drawings show the design on both sides.

that remains today are two small stone churches, Teaghlach Éinne and Teampall Bheanáin, the stunt of a once lofty round tower and fragments of an inscribed stone cross. It is claimed that Enda's monastic 'city' extended from Teaghlach Éinne to Teampall Bheanáin. However these two surviving buildings probably stood apart from the main monastery, a fact that saved them from destruction when Cromwell's soldiers destroyed all of the other buildings to provide material for the fortification of Arkyne Castle near Killeany Harbour in the 17th century.

Teaghlach Éinne is situated in an ancient graveyard among the sandhills at the eastern end of An Trá Mór. This graveyard is reputed to be the burial place of Enda and over a hundred of his followers and it still serves as a cemetery for the people of the nearby villages.

Teampall Bheanáin overlooks the bay from a remarkable hilltop position. It is a tiny church, hardly fifteen feet in its internal length, and is constructed from massive stone slabs. Regarded as the smallest church in Europe, it is orientated from North to South in contrast with all the other Aran churches which are orientated East to West. Nearby are the ruins of a number of clochans, or beehive huts, and the remnant of a wall which may once have surrounded a cathair or monastic settlement.

The stump of a round tower can be seen in a field near the sheltered harbour. This tower is said to have been sixty metres high and to have been blown down in a storm in the late 17th century. Elaborately carved sections of the shaft of a cross, which were found near this site, stand in a field to the east of the tower.

Enda's monastery flourished for over five hundred years after the death of the saint. Many of the great saints of the early Irish church including Brendan the Navigator and Kieran of Clonmacnoise, studied there and monks from this foundation were to be found preaching the gospel in all parts of Europe during the Dark Ages. In the 11th century the monastery suffered a succession of disasters. It was almost destroyed by fire in 1020 A.D. and was raised by Vikings in 1017 A.D. and 1081 A.D. In time the community became apathetic and its rule lax until the arrival of Franciscan monks in the 15th century. The last recorded Abbot of Killeany died in 1400 A.D. but the monastery seems to have lived on, surviving the reign of Henry VIII when most of the Irish monasteries were suppressed, and to have continued its work until 1586 when it too was dissolved by his daughter Elizabeth I.

Many legends concerning miraculous events in the life of Enda are still related. One such story from the island's folklore concerns the visit of St. Colmcille to Killeany where he studied under Enda's discipline. Colmcille loved the peace and beauty of Aran and he asked Enda for a plot of ground on which he might build a cell. Enda refused feeling that Colmcille's fame would lead to his own name being forgotten. He feared that Aran would be known thereafter as Colmcille's island. Colmcille eventually persuaded Enda to allow him to take just as much land as his cloak would cover. When the cloak was spread on the ground it began to stretch and stretch. Enda snatched it up lest it cover the whole of his island. Colmcille became violently angry and he laid a curse on the island which was never to be lifted. He declared that strangers and foreigners would overrun the islands; that the land would not yield a harvest without great labour; that the cows would not produce milk in quantity; that turf would never be found there. Enda's greatest fear also came to pass for even today a greater devotion exists to St. Colmcille on the islands than to any other saint.

ONAGHT

The second greatest monastic settlement on Inishmore is known as the Seven Churches and it is found at Onaght in the western part of the island. It is unlikely that there ever were seven churches on this site for all that now remains are the substantial ruins of two churches and a number of domestic buildings. This monastery, like that at Killeany, occupies good land with a permanent supply of fresh water. A stream runs through the little valley where it is located and some of the deepest soil on Inishmore can be found there.

The older of the two churches dates from the 8th century and is dedicated to St. Brecan. When first built it was similar in size to Teaghlach Éinne but it was enlarged over the centuries and the west gable clearly shows the original dimensions. St. Brecan was renowned for his piety and for the severity of his rule but little is known of the details of his life. He is said to have been a monk in the Killeany community and to have succeeded Enda as Abbot but his reason for moving to Onaght remains a mystery.

Teampall A'Phoill, 'The Church of the Hollow' is situated a few metres further up the valley. It is a 15th century structure which was probably used as an ordinary parish church until relatively recent times. Located near these churches are remains of five rectangular domestic buildings. They date from various periods and some of them were built as late as the 16th century.

Within the monastic enclosure are a number of graves, regarded as the last resting place of Brendan and some of his monks. The site also contains several inscribed stones and a portion of the shaft of a cross.

* * *

Between the two major sites of Killeany and Onaght are the ruins of numerous other Early Christian structures. The most notable of these is Teampall an Ceathrar Alainn, 'The Church of the Four Comely Saints' situated south of the main road near the village of Cowrugh. The four saints mentioned in the dedication are Fursey, Brendan of Birr, Conall and Berchan. There are no records to explain why the church is dedicated to these saints nor do we know why they were described as An Ceathrar Alainn. South of this church, in a nearby field, is a holy well chosen by Synge as the supposed location of his play *The Well of the Saints.* A number of other churches are also found on Inishmore. Teampall MacDuach, dedicated to St. Colman a patron of sailors, and Teampall na Naomh, of which little is known, are both situated near the village of Kilmurvey. In the district of Mainistir, about one and a half kilometres west of Kilronan are Teampall Chiaráin, a church that originated in the Golden Age and was enlarged to its present substantial size in the Medieval period. This St. Chiaráin, a disciple of Enda's, is believed to be the founder of one of the greatest monasteries in Ireland – at Clonmacnoise. Some distance west of this is the much smaller Teampall Asurnai, thought to be dedicated to a female saint, Soarney, though this is in no way certain.

INISHMAAN

Inishmaan seems never to have supported a major monastic community though a complex of ruins exists on fertile land near the centre of the island, which indicates that a monastery may once have occupied the site. Teampall na Seacht mic Righ, of which only the foundations remain, commemorates seven brothers, of noble birth, who came here as hermits. Teampall Muire nearby, was a late medieval building which served as a parish

Above – Teampall a'Phoill – The Church of the Hollow. One of the two churches at the 'Seven Churches' monastic site on Inishmore. This 15th century structure stands at the head of a fertile well watered valley. Nearby are the remains of rectangular domestic buildings from about the same period.

Left – Clochan na Carraige, Inishmore, 1885, before restoration. This is a typical example of a dry stone beehive hut. Such clochan's were probably the domestic dwellings in the Aran monastic enclosure in the early Christian period.

church for over 500 years. Near the east shore of this island stands the well preserved remains of a small church known as Kilcanaragh, though the derivation of the name is not now known.

INISHEER

On Inisheer the remains of several churches can be seen though tradition maintains that others have been lost on the shifting sand dunes at the north end of the island. Some traces of the foundations of a church, Cill na Eacht nIníon, the Church of the Seven Daughters, can be seen near the eastern side of the island. Nothing is known of these seven female saints but it is almost certain that they have no connection with the seven princes commemorated on Inishmaan.

Teampall Chaomháin, the Church of St. Cavan, is much better preserved. Like Teaghlach Éinne on Inishmore it stands in a graveyard among the sand dunes and is in constant danger of being covered completely by the movement of the sands. St. Cavan is believed to have been a brother of St. Kevin of Glendalough. A considerable devotion towards him still exists on Inisheer and 'Cavan' is a common Christian name for boys on the island. Teampall Ghobnait (or Kilgobnet, the Church of St. Gobnet), another small church, is dedicated to a female saint who is venerated in Munster and who found refuge for a time on Inisheer.

Left — Teampall Bheanáin — the tiny hilltop church dedicated to St. Benan. The walls are built of massive blocks of stone.

Teampall MacDuach near Kilmurvey Inishmore is dedicated to
St. Colman MacDuach. The very fine medieval arch was part of an
extension in the Romanesque style.

conquest of aran

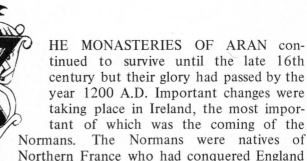

HE MONASTERIES OF ARAN continued to survive until the late 16th century but their glory had passed by the year 1200 A.D. Important changes were taking place in Ireland, the most important of which was the coming of the Normans. The Normans were natives of Northern France who had conquered England after the Battle of Hastings in 1066 and had settled there. They were soldiers and adventurers, skilled in warfare and highly organised under a single king. Ireland, by contrast, was a patchwork of tiny kingdoms ruled over in name only by a High King or Árd Rí. The Aran Islands were an almost independent territory ruled by the McTeige O'Briens, a branch of the powerful O'Brien family of Co. Clare.

Around the middle of the 12th century Dermot MacMurrough, King of Leinster was deprived of his territory after he had quarrelled with the Árd Rí and another Irish chieftain, O'Rourke of Breifne. Dermot fled to England where he recruited a band of Norman knights and footsoldiers. With this force he returned to Ireland in 1169 A.D. and rapidly conquered the fertile lands around the old Viking towns of Waterford, Wexford and Dublin. Dermot died leaving the Norman knights in possession of large tracts of land. Henry II, King of England, the overlord of the Normans, was crowned as King of Ireland.

The Norman's influence was largely confined to the east of the country and it was not until the 14th century that they attempted to subdue the wild and isolated west coast. The Lord Justice, one of the king's deputies, sailed up the west coast in 1334. Ancient records show that he plundered Inishmore, which, along with Inisheer had a considerable population at this time. It is thought that Inishmaan may have been uninhabited, except for a few monks or hermits.

The O'Brien's were allowed to continue as lords of the islands because the walled city of Galway had come to depend on their goodwill as masters of Galway Bay. The O'Brien's accepted an annual payment from the citizens for controlling piracy and for not interfering with trade to and from the city. This arrangement suited both parties and they tolerated one another in peace. The O'Brien's built a fortified tower house within the walls of Dun Formna. They may also have built a small castle at Killeany and they were the patrons of the Franciscan monastery established there in 1480. The mainland of Ireland was less peaceful than the islands during the 14th, 15th and 16th centuries with the Norman-English gradually increasing their influence. Certain branches of the Gaelic clans were prepared to recognise the English King as their overlord in order to gain control of the clan lands with his support. Such a conflict developed in 1584 among the O'Flaherty's of west Galway which resulted in the clan chief and his followers fleeing to Aran where they found refuge with the O'Brien's. The victorious branch of the clan, who had been supported by the English, pursued the fugitives and finally defeated them and their allies the O'Brien's. The Aran Islands passed into the hands of the O'Flaherty's. The reign of the O'Brien's was at an end, though they were to make repeated efforts to regain their lost lands.

The O'Brien's appealed to the Crown, and a Commission was established in Galway city in 1587 to decide on the ownership of the islands. The government, however, decided to annex the islands which they saw as being of strategic importance in the defence of the kingdom against French and Spanish enemies. They argued that the islands were monastery land and that, as the monasteries of Ireland and England had been suppressed by law and their lands taken over by the crown, the islands were the rightful property of the Queen. In the Government view neither the O'Briens or the O'Flahertys could be trusted and so the islands were granted to John Rawson of Athlone on condition that he kept the garrison of soldiers there. Thus the ownership of the land of Aran passed from those who lived on it and worked it. John Rawson, believed to have been the builder of Arkyne

Castle, sold the islands to the Lynch family of Galway in 1588.

Seventeenth century Ireland was a country ravaged by almost continuous warfare. By the middle of the century the battle lines were being drawn on a new basis, that of religion. Some of the native Irish chiefs and the Anglo-Norman lords, in 1642, united in the Confederation of Kilkenny, the aim of which was the restoration of the Catholic religion. Their opponent, Cromwell, the Lord Protector of England, landed in Dublin in 1649. He waged total war on his enemies, capturing the major towns and laying waste the countryside. Tens of thousands of civilians were given the option "to Hell or Connaught" and were driven westward by his victorious armies. The fertile lands which they vacated were given to planters from England and Scotland. It seems probable that some of the dispossessed who were forced to cross the Shannon into Connaught may have settled on the islands at this time.

The Marquis of Clanrickarde, one of the leaders on the Irish side, hoped that the tide could be turned if his French allies sent troops to Ireland as they had promised. He garrisoned the Aran Islands in order to preserve a point of entry for this expected aid. Sir Robert Lynch, the owner of the islands, was given the title of Commander-in-chief and he was supplied with 200 soldiers. Arkyne castle was fortified and Inishmore was placed on a war footing. The French force failed to arrive and the Irish were repeatedly defeated. Galway City fell to the Cromwellians in December 1650, though seven hundred officers and men from its garrison escaped to Inishboffin.

The small Aran garrison surrendered and a body of Cromwell's troops were sent to hold down the island and to strengthen Arkyne Castle. They demolished a number of ancient churches of St. Enda's monastery and used the stone as building material. While they were engaged on this work, in 1652, the Irish troops from Inishboffin took them by surprise and regained control of Arkyne. A Cromwellian force of 1300 men, under the command of General Reynolds laid siege to Arkyne. The garrison surrendered within a week and were allowed to take ship for the continent. Sir Robert Lynch was declared a traitor and his lands forfeit. The islands became the property of a Cromwellian, Erasmus Smith.

During the next decade the Government strengthened the defences of Arkyne Castle and made use of it as a prison camp for Catholic priests awaiting deportation to the West Indies. A

The 15th century O'Brien Castle at Inisheer.

garrison was maintained on the islands but in the more peaceful era of the 18th century the fortifications at Arkyne were allowed to crumble and the number of men stationed there dwindled. In the meantime the islands changed hands on several occasions. Erasmus Smith sold his interest to the Butler's of Ormond. Richard Butler received the title Earl of Aran in 1662 but this family soon parted with the land and those who later bore the title had no connection with Aran.

During the 18th and 19th centuries the islands were owned by a succession of absentee landlords whose sole interest was the income they received from rent. Agents, who were placed in charge, extracted huge rents from the island tenants whose living conditions worsened rapidly. By the early 19th century the tenants were paying over £2,000 per annum in rent to their landlord, a huge sum in the values of the time, which must have severely strained the meagre resources of Aran.

The Fitzmaurice's of Galway City owned the islands for a time but lost them to the Digby family of Co. Kildare early in the 19th century on a mortgage which they failed to repay. In 1870 Elizabeth Digby married and became Countess of Howth and the ownership of Aran passed to her two surviving daughters, under her marriage settlement. Under the Land Acts of 1881 and 1882, tenants obtained the right to sell their interest in the land, and later were able to buy out their holdings under special purchase schemes. As a result, in the first two decades of the 20th century, most of the island families had acquired the ownership of their land.

A heavy load. A farmyard at Inishmaan.

THE OARSMEN'S SONG

It's only twice a week she comes
How we look forward to that day.
Like some good omen to our homes
She blows her note across the bay.
There's bread in chests and oil in drums,
A wardrobe and a mattress
A box of nibs, a card of combs,
And a mail bag full of letters.

As black and hollow as huge pods,
The currachs dandle on the wave,
Wild winch and pulley lower the goods,
The sailors shout, the seagulls rave.
There's whitewash brushes, bags of nails,
With bottled gas and liquor,
Long iron gates, enamel pails,
And a hamper made of wicker.

What we can't load we float behind —
Slim planks for rafters, boards for floors,
Back from the steamer to the land
We're lying heavy on the oars:
With tins of polish, panes of glass,
And shafts for scythes and shafts for spades,
A pram, a cot, a plastic bath,
And shaving soap and razor blades.

Seamus Heaney

aran in the 19th.century

HE FARM CLUSTER, or clachan in Irish, is the dominant settlement form of the Aran Islands. The cluster, referred to locally as a 'village', is a group of farmer's dwelling houses and outbuildings sited close together. It contrasts strongly with the dispersed form of settlement found elsewhere in Ireland where each dwelling house stands at the centre of its farm, often a mile or more from its nearest neighbour. A typical clachan contains two to fifteen houses, irregularly grouped together without a main street, village green or market place. It usually does not have any services such as shop, pub, church or school though many of the Aran clachans have acquired one or more of these.

This type of settlement has deep roots in Irish history, going back almost to Celtic times. Like the great duns of Aran, each clachan housed a number of families, who held the surrounding land in common ownership. A fence enclosed a large tract of arable land known as the Infield where each individual farmer had a number of strips to grow crops. The unfenced pasture or rough grazing owned by the group was called the Outfield and each farmer was entitled to graze a number of animals on this.

Clachans were common in many parts of Ireland before the Great Famine of the 1840's. Thousands of people who were forced to move westwards into Connaught by Cromwell's armies in the seventeenth century settled in such groupings on the coasts of Galway and Mayo. Living close together gave the members of the group a sense of security and solidarity as they attempted to make a new life in a harsh environment. Some of the Aran 'villages' probably had their origins in this movement. After the famine, land holding was re-organised in the more fertile parts of Ireland and farm clusters were broken up in favour of isolated family dwellings, each of which stood on its own compact farm. On the west coast, however, the clachan remains though the communal ownership of land has almost totally disappeared.

Many clachans, and former clachans, in different parts of the country, contain the word "Bally" as an element in their place-names. "Bally" is derived from the Irish word "Baile" meaning a townland division and its cluster. The villages of Inishmaan almost all have names which include this element such as Ballintemple or Kimbally as do three of the four villages in Inisheer. Many of the Inishmore villages' names date from the monastic period, Killeany, Kilronan and Kilmurvey being examples, while others take their names from landscape features such as Sruthán, a stream, or Bungowla, the bottom of the fork.

The clachan type of settlement is a concrete expression of the close blood links and marriage links which exist on the Aran Islands. The surname Hernon embraces a majority of those living in Kilmurvey and Cooke is similarly associated with Bungowla and Gill with Killeany. Where related families live in close proximity to one another they are in a position to aid one another in their daily work or in a crisis. This giving of "cabhair" or help, often described as "cooring", depends not on the payment of money for work performed but rather on a return of the favour at the appropriate time. Tasks such as harvesting of rye or the burning of kelp, requiring a number of workers, can be carried out in this way. The giving and receiving of such aid is an important aspect of social organisation.

Almost all of the Aran clusters are found in the north, or leeside of the slopes. The exception, Gort na gCapall, is situated in the low neck of land between the two ridges of Inishmore where shelter is not available in any case. No dwelling houses are located on the crags at the back of the islands though a shed or barn can be seen in some isolated fields.

Other than in the case of Gort na gCapall the clusters are found on one of the two broad terraces midway between summit and shore. These broad terraces are backed by thick bands of shale and each is well watered by springs. The limited number of springs

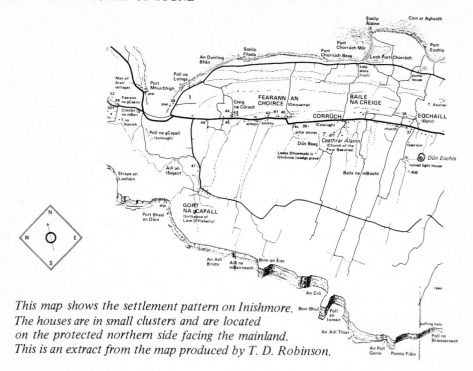

This map shows the settlement pattern on Inishmore.
The houses are in small clusters and are located
on the protected northern side facing the mainland.
This is an extract from the map produced by T. D. Robinson.

Where shore and land meet at Inisheer.

available is an added reason for the clustering of houses. Down-slope of the houses are the patches of arable land and pasture while upslope on the hilltops and the crags are the winter pastures. The carrying of water to the livestock in summer is an easy down-hill journey performed by the women while the men are busily engaged in fishing. The more difficult uphill journey in winter is regarded as a man's job.

In the pre-Famine period each Aran cluster consisted of 10 to 15 dwellings. The pattern of work moved up and down the slope with the seasons rather than along the slope. Thus the people living in a clachan were more concerned with the sea, the shore and the pasture and tillage below and the winter grazing above them than with the neighbouring clusters on the same terrace. The independence of each clachan is shown by the fact that the settlement of Iarairne was not even connected by road with the others, at the time the first detailed maps were completed in 1839. In the post-Famine period many of the clusters have shrunk, some, like Ballindun on Inishmaan, being reduced to two occupied houses. With the passage of time the individual clusters have been 'stretched' as new houses have been built along the road. Inish-maan, viewed from the sea, presents a continuous line of houses rather than a number of distinct villages. The number of 'villages' on Inishmore varies from ten to fourteen depending on whether, one regards the smaller clusters as being independent of or merged with the larger.

On Aran settlement has tended to move downslope. New houses are generally taller than the old and their builders seek a lower more sheltered site. The ten houses in the 'village' of Sruthán on Inishmore were all sited above the road in pre-famine days but the whole village is now situated below the road. Killeany and Kilronan are larger than the other Aran settlements and have a wider range of functions than the traditional clachans. Killeany grew up around the 14th century Franciscan Friary and Arkyne Castle. Its sheltered harbour, protected by the castle, made it the 'capital' of the islands, and of West Connacht, for several centuries. The people of Killeany at that time were soldiers, sailors and government officials rather than farmers. They were divorced from the land as was the fishing community which grew up around the harbour. The castle and its garrison have long since gone but the people of Killeany are still less tied to the land than the other islanders. Kilronan resulted from the merging of two farm clusters along the main road early in the 19th century.

After the famine a newly built pier made it more important than Killeany. A courthouse, a police barracks and a coastguard station were sited there, giving it a completely different character to the other Inishmore clusters.

POPULATION

The population of Ireland increased rapidly during the second half of the eighteenth century. The country as a whole made little progress in industry or trade during this time. Farming was the only means of providing a living for this expanding population, especially on the isolated and underdeveloped west coast. Pressure on the land became more severe with each succeeding generation. The rule of primogeniture, that is inheritance by the first born, had never been observed in Ireland. A farmer would divide his land between all of his surviving children rather than pass it on to his eldest son and so, quite large farms were reduced to a collection of individually owned patches within a generation or two. The tenants who farmed such patches on Aran were rack-rented by their landlords. By the beginning of the 19th century the population of the islands had risen to 2,400; the vast majority of these had to eke out a living from a few rocky fields, while paying a total rental of over £2,000 per annum to an absentee landlord. This huge rent was often too great a burden on the tenants, who would fall into arrears. J. M. Synge witnessed the eviction of several Inishmaan farmers for non-payment of rent.

"Two recent attempts to carry out evictions on the island came to nothing, for each time a sudden storm rose, by, it is said, the power of a native witch, when the steamer was approaching, and made it impossible to land.

This morning, however, broke beneath a clear sky of June and when I came into the open air the sea and rocks were shining with wonderful brilliancy. Groups of men, dressed in their holiday clothes, were standing about, talking with anger and fear, yet showing a lurking satisfaction at the thought of the dramatic pageant that was to break the silence of the seas.

About half-past nine the steamer came in sight on the narrow line of sea-horizon that is seen in the centre of the bay, and immediately a last effort was made to hide the cows and sheep of the families that were most in debt.

Till this year no one on the island would consent to act as bailiff, so that it was impossible to identify the cattle of the

A typical Aran farm cluster of the late 19th century. The thatch roof cottages have small deep set windows. The stone walled fields are intensively tilled with 'lazy beds'.

defaulters. Now, however, a man of the name of Patrick has sold his honour, and the effort of concealment is practically futile.

This falling away from the ancient loyalty of the island has caused intense indignation and early yesterday morning, while I was dreaming on the Dun, this letter was nailed on the doorpost of the chapel:

'Patrick, the devil, a revolver is waiting for you. If you are missed with the first shot, there will be five more that will hit you.

'Any man that will talk with you, or work with you, or drink a pint of porter in your shop, will be done with the same way as yourself.'

As the steamer drew near I moved down with the men to watch the arrival, though no one went further than about a mile from the shore.

Two curaghs from Kilronan with a man who was to give help in identifying the cottages, the doctor, and the relieving officer, were drifting with the tide, unwilling to come to land without the support of the larger party. When the anchor had been thrown it gave me a strange throb of pain to see the boats being lowered, and the sunshine gleaming on the rifles and helmets of the constabulary who crowded into them.

Once on shore the men were formed in close marching order, a word was given, and the heavy rhythm of their boots came up over the rocks. We were collected in two straggling bands on either side of the roadway, and a few moments later the body of magnificent armed men passed close to us, followed by a low rabble, who had been brought to act as drivers for the sheriff.

After my weeks spent among primitive men this glimpse of the newer types of humanity was not reassuring. Yet these mechanical police, with the commonplace agents and sheriffs, and the rabble they had hired, represented aptly enough the civilization for which the homes of the island were to be desecrated.

A stop was made at one of the first cottages in the village, and the day's work began. Here, however, and at the next cottage, a compromise was made, as some relatives came up at the last moment and lent the money that was needed to gain a respite.

In another case a girl was ill in the house, so the doctor interposed, and the people were allowed to remain after a merely formal eviction. About midday, however, a house was reached where there was no pretext for mercy, and no money could be procured. At a sign from the sheriff the work of carrying out the

beds and utensils was begun in the middle of a crowd of natives who looked on in absolute silence, broken only by the wild imprecations of the woman of the house. She belonged to one of the most primitive families on the island, and she shook with un-controllable fury as she saw the strange armed men who spoke a language she could not understand driving her from the hearth she had brooded on for thirty years. For these people the outrage to the hearth is the supreme catastrophe. They live here in a world of grey, where there are wild rains and mists every week in the year, and their warm chimney corners, filled with children and young girls, grow into the consciousness of each family in a way it is not easy to understand in more civilized places.

The outrage to a tomb in China probably gives no greater shock to the Chinese than the outrage to a hearth in Inishmaan gives to the people.

When the few trifles had been carried out, and the door blocked with stones, the old woman sat down by the threshold and covered her head with her shawl.

Five or six other women who lived close by sat down in a circle round her, with mute sympathy. Then the crowd moved on with the police to another cottage where the same scene was to take place, and left the group of desolate women sitting by the hovel.

There were still no clouds in the sky, and the heat was intense. The police when not in motion lay sweating and gasping under the walls with their tunics unbuttoned. They were not attractive, and I kept comparing them with the islandmen, who walked up and down as cool and fresh-looking as the sea-gulls.

When the last eviction had been carried out a division was made: half the party went off with the bailiff to search the inner plain of the island for the cattle that had been hidden in the morning, the other half remained on the village road to guard some pigs that had already been taken possession of.

After a while two of these pigs escaped from the drivers and began a wild race up and down the narrow road. The people shrieked and howled to increase their terror, and at last some of them became so excited that the police thought it time to inter-fere. They drew up in double line opposite the mouth of a blind laneway where the animals had been shut up. A moment later the shrieking began again in the west and the two pigs came in sight, rushing down the middle of the road with the drivers behind them.

They reached the line of the police. There was a slight scuffle, and then the pigs continued their mad rush to the east, leaving three policemen lying in the dust.

The satisfaction of the people was immense. They shrieked and hugged each other with delight, and it is likely that they will hand down these animals for generations in the tradition of the island.

Two hours later the other party returned, driving three lean cows before them, and a start was made for the slip. At the public-house the policemen were given a drink while the dense crowd that was following waited in the lane. The island bull happened to be in a field close by, and he became wildly excited at the sight of the cows and of the strangely dressed men. Two young islanders sidled up to me in a moment or two as I was resting on a wall, and one of them whispered in my ear:

'Do you think they could take fines of us if we let out the bull on them?'

In face of the crowd of women and children, I could only say it was probable, and they slunk off.

At the slip there was a good deal of bargaining, which ended in all the cattle being given back to their owners. It was plainly of no use to take them away, as they were worth nothing.

When the last policeman had embarked, an old woman came forward from the crowd and, mounting on a rock near the slip, began a fierce rhapsody in Gaelic, pointing at the bailiff and waving her withered arms with extraordinary rage.

'This man is my own son,' she said; 'it is I that ought to know him. He is the first ruffian in the whole big world.'

Then she gave an account of his life, coloured with a vindictive fury I cannot reproduce. As she went on the excitement became so intense I thought the man would be stoned before he could get back to his cottage.

On these islands the women live only for their children, and it is hard to estimate the power of the impulse that made this old woman stand out and curse her son.

In the fury of her speech I seem to look again into the strange reticent temperament of the islanders, and to feel the passionate spirit that expresses itself, at odd moments only, with magnificent words and gestures."

In such conditions the potato became the key to survival. It had been introduced into Ireland from the "New World" about the year 1600 A.D. It proved to be an ideal crop in the damp climate and produced good yields even from poor soils. It became the stable food of the people in the late 18th century and though a diet of potatoes and milk may have been monotonous it provided enough nourishment to sustain life. The sale of a calf or pig served to pay the rent and the farmer and his family subsisted on the produce of their potato patch. Fishermen and labourers who had not inherited land managed to sub-let a plot for a period of eleven months to grow a crop of potatoes. This practice was known as taking land on conacre.

A man who acquired land, through inheritance or rental, felt confident that he could support a family and so, tended to marry while still very young. The large families of such youthful marriages had increased the population of Aran to 3,521 by the year 1841. The islands, especially Inishmore, were overpopulated and the stage was set for disaster. Blight, a fungus that blackens the potato and renders it inedible struck the crop for the first time during the 1820's. It was to re-appear at regular intervals during the century leaving a trail of death and disease in its wake. The loss of the potato crop was the greatest disaster that could befall the hard pressed tenants.

The pressure which population exerted on resources in the late 19th century can be seen in the landscape of Inisheer, which was itself much less crowded than Inishmore.

In the following extract from Liam O'Flaherty's novel *Famine,* the Kilmartin family discover that potato blight is sweeping through their crop.

ANOTHER VIOLENT STORM CAME ON the last day of the month. They did not trouble greatly about this one, since the first had done no damage. Even so, a rumour got abroad that the blight had struck in the County Cork. Would it come this far? Every day, they anxiously inspected the crop. But the days passed without any sign of the evil. The potatoes that were dug for food still remained wholesome. It promised to be a miraculous crop. Even Mary began to take courage. And then, on the fifteenth of July, the bolt fell from the heavens.

When old Kilmartin came into his yard shortly after dawn on that day, he looked up the Valley and saw a white cloud standing above the Black Lake. It was like a great mound of snow, hanging by an invisible chain, above the mountain peaks. It was dazzling white in the glare of the rising sun.

"Merciful God!" he said. "What can that be?"

The rest of the sky was as clear as crystal. The old man stared at it in awe for some time. Then he ran into the house and called out the family to look at it. Mary and Thomsy came out. They were as startled as the old man.

"Did you ever see anything like that?" the old man said.

"Never in my natural," said Thomsy. "It's like a....."

"Snow," Mary said. "It's like a big heap of snow."

"How could it be snow?" said the old man. "And this the middle of summer? It's a miracle."

"Or would it be a bad sign. God between us and harm?" said Thomsy.

Other people came from their cabins and stared at the cloud. There was a peculiar silence in the Valley. The air was as heavy as a drug. There was not a breath of wind. The birds did not sing. And then, as the people watched, the cloud began to move lazily down upon the Valley. It spread out on either side, lost its form and polluted the atmosphere which became full of a whitish vapour, through which the sun's rays glistened; so that it seemed that a fine rain of tiny whitish particles of dust was gently falling from the sky. Gradually a sulphurous stench affected the senses of those who watched. It was like the smell of foul water in a sewer. Yet, there was no moisture and the stench left an aris feeling in the nostrils. Even the animals were affected by it. Dogs sat up on their haunches and howled. Not a bird was to be seen, although there had been flocks of crows and starlings about on the previous day. Then, indeed, terror seized the people and a loud wailing broke out from the cabins, as the cloud overspread the whole Valley, shutting out the sun completely.

All this time, the whole Kilmartin family had remained in the yard. Mary clutched the baby in her arms. Nobody thought of preparing breakfast, although the morning was now well advanced. It was only when the wailing began and Maggie joined in it, that Mary came to her senses and said:

"Don't frighten the child with your whining. There's no harm done yet. Hold the baby, mother, while I get breakfast ready."

"True for you," said the old man. "There's no harm done yet. Into the house, all of you. Pooh! Afraid of a fog, is it?" Maggie stopped crying, but she went back to bed and closed the door of her room. The others made an attempt to be cheerful. Like people who feel the oncoming panic of despair, they gave voice to expressions of optimism, which they knew to be false.

"I often saw fogs heavier than that," Ellen Gleeson said, as she rocked the baby in the hearth corner.

"As heavy as that?" said Thomsy. "Sure that's not a heavy fog. I saw a fog once that was as thick as night. You can see to the end of the yard in this one."

"You can see farther," said the old man. "On the south side there, you can see as far as Patsy O'Hanlon's house. It's not a thick fog. It's funny the smell that comes from fogs."

"I never smelt a fog before like that," said Mary. "It must be a new kind of fog. But a fog can do no harm in any case. If it was rain now, that would be a different story. Rain might rot the potatoes and they..."

"Nothing will rot the potatoes," said the old man. "God forgive you for saying such a thing."

Mary cooked some Indian meal and turnips, of which a few still remained. While they were eating, a further astonishing thing happened. The sky cleared almost instantaneously. The sun shone brilliantly. Yet this change, which should have cheered the watchers, only increased their awe, for the stench still remained. They all stopped eating. The old man got to his feet. He reached for his hat and fumbled with it, looking about him at the others with the expression of a small boy who has committed some offence of which he is ashamed.

"Blood an ouns!" Thomsy said, jumping to his feet.

With his mouth wide open, he stared at the old man. Then they both clapped their hats on their heads and rushed from the house. Mary ran to the cradle, picked up the child and pressed it to her bosom.

"What ails ye?" her mother said.

Maggie began to wail in the bedroom. All the colour had gone from Mary's cheeks and her eyes seemed to have enlarged. She handed the baby to her mother and whispered:

"I'm going out to look at the gardens."

Thomsy and the old man, one after the other and with their hands behind their backs, were walking slowly down towards the potato gardens, still shining in all the glory of their dark-green foliage, under the radiant sun. But the stench was now terrible. In single file, they came to the first garden and leaned over the stone fence close together, staring at the plants.

Uttering shriek after shriek, he climbed over the fence, fumbling so much that he dislodged several stones. He strode through the stalks, that came up to his waist, across the ridges, until he came to the affected spot. The stench was now that of active corruption. The old man seized the stalks that were marked with spots and began to pull them. The leaves withered when he touched them and the stalks snapped like rotten wood. But the potatoes clinging to the uprooted stalks were whole. The old man dug into several of them with his nails.

"They're not rotten," he cried, laughing hysterically. "Come on, Thomsy. Pull the stalks that are rotten. We must stop it spreading."

Excited by the old man's frenzy, Thomsy also climbed over the fence and waddled through the stalks, but he halted when he was a few yards from the old man who was pulling feverishly and shouting. The old man was now surrounded by a widening lake of spots.

"Sure, it's flying all over the garden," said Thomsy. "Look, man. It's all round you. You can't stop it."

"What's that?" said the old man, raising his head.

He looked all round him pathetically. Then his mouth fell open and he stood up straight. His hands dropped to his sides.

"You're right," he said faintly. "It's the hand of God. God's will be done."

Thereupon he crossed himself and bowed his head. Not troubling even to collect the potatoes he had pulled up with the stalks, he marched slowly back to the fence, carelessly trampling over the stalks that were still untouched. Mary turned away from the fence as he approached. She began to walk back to the house.

The wailing was now general all over the Valley.

"They're alright," said the old man. "There's nothing on them."

"Whist!" said Thomsy. "What's that I hear?"

Towards the north, in the direction towards which Thomsy pointed, Mary and the old man saw people looking over fences, just as they themselves were doing. These people had begun to wail. In this wailing there was a note of utter despair. There was no anger in it, no power, not even an appeal for mercy. It was just like the death groan of a mortally wounded person, groaning in horror of inevitable death.

"It's the blight," Mary whispered. "Oh! God in Heaven!"

"Look," gasped the old man through his teeth. "Look at it. It's the devil. It's the devil himself."

With outstretched hand, that trembled as if palsied, he pointed to a little hollow about ten yards within the fence. Here the growth was particularly luxuriant and the branches of the potato stalks were matted as thickly as a carpet. Mary and Thomsy followed the direction of his hand and while he babbled foolishly they saw the evil appear on the leaves. A group of little brown spots had appeared and they spread, as if by magic, while they watched. It was just like the movement of an incoming tide over a flat, sandy shore. It was a rain of spots, spreading rapidly in all directions. "Oh! God Almighty!" Thomsy cried. "Save us, oh, Lord! Jesus! Mary and Joseph!"

Cormorants, Inishmore.

The Famine, more correctly the Great Hunger, of the 1840's brought catastrophe on the country as a whole. Blight, aided by bad weather, completely destroyed the crop in 1845, 1846 and 1847. One million people died of hunger and famine fever and a million others fled the country, emigrating to the industrial cities of England and Scotland, and especially, to the United States.

The Aran Islands, and the west coast in general, seem to have escaped the worst effects of the disaster. The population of Inishmore decreased but the percentage decline was far less than the national average. The number of people living on Inishmaan and Inisheer actually increased during the decade. These islands were less crowded than Inishmore and they may even have provided refuge for people from the mainland. The availability of food from the sea and the shore blunted the effects of crop failure on all three islands.

POPULATION FIGURES

Year	Inisheer	Inishmaan	Inishmore	Total
1812				2,400
1821	421	387	2,285	3,093
1831				3,191
1841	456	473	2,592	3,521
1851	518	503	2,312	3,333
1861	532	478	2,289	3,299
1871	495	433	2,122	3,050
1881	497	473	2,193	3,163
1891	455	456	1,996	2,907
1901	483	421	1,959	2,863

Aran was not to fare so well during the remainder of the century. Partial failures of the potato crop occurred on the west coast in 1879 and 1889 causing great suffering and hardship once more. The morale of the people could not withstand such repeated blows. Emigration, a trickle since the 1820's and a steady stream since the 1840's, now became a flood as the young departed in search of a more promising life abroad. The community lost confidence in its own ability to survive. Farmers tried to keep their farms intact to pass on to one son when the others would all have departed. Men were slow to enter into marriage waiting cautiously until they would have the security of ownership before taking a partner. Many waited too long and failed to marry at all.

Name and Description of Parishes, &c.	Inhabited Houses.	By how many Families occupied.	Houses now building	Families chiefly employed in Agriculture	Families chiefly employed in Trade, Manufactures & Handic.	All other Families not comprised in the two preceding classes	Males.	Females.
The three Islands of Arran, Half Barony and Parish of Arran, viz.								
Island of Eniseer,	47	47	4	46	-	1	141	154
Island of Enismane,	51	55	3	51	4	-	164	156
Killeany Village in Great Island	78	82	2	78	4	-	249	211
Kilronan, ditto,	52	52	2	48	4	-	191	169
Manister, ditto,	9	9	1	9	-	-	26	25
Oghill, ditto,	24	24	-	20	3	1	64	54
Ballinacreggy, ditto,	22	22	2	19	3	-	67	63
Oat-quarter, ditto,	19	19	-	17	2	-	60	45
Gorthnagapple ditto,	18	18	1	18	-	-	49	53
Kilmurry, ditto,	15	15	-	15	-	-	43	50
Corrig, ditto,	10	10	-	10	-	-	28	38
Onaught, ditto,	19	19	1	19	-	-	59	51
Cregaherean, ditto,	20	20	-	20	-	-	64	63
Bungowley, ditto,	11	11	-	11	-	-	39	24
Total,	395	400	17	381	20	2	1244	1156

Census of the Aran Islands 1812.

The burial memorials, found in groups, along the roadways of Inishmore, remain a mystery to scholars. The inscriptions which commemorate individuals, date from the late 18th and early 19th centuries but it is believed that mounds of stones existed on these sites long before the monuments were cemented and decorated with crosses and plaques in the early 19th century.

As each succeeding generation of young people left, the islands developed a society of aged spinsters and bachelors.

Inishmore has suffered most in the general decline. The villages of Killeany and Kilronan contributed largely to this and their inhabitants depended on the fishing industry which slumped disastrously in the late 19th century. The other islands fared better, probably because they have always had a more equal balance between their populations and available resources.

THE IRISH LANGUAGE

By the year 1800 A.D. the Irish language was being abandoned as the vernacular, or daily spoken language, of the majority of Irish men. English was spoken in the homes of the prosperous and Irish was regarded as the language of the poor and the backward. The number of Irish speakers did increase in the country as a whole between the years 1800 and 1840 but only because the population, particularly the poorer sections, increased rapidly during this period. The repeated famines after 1840 affected the poor more than any other class and so dealt a death blow to their language. From 1870 onwards the rate of emigration from the Irish speaking counties of the west was far higher than the national average.

By 1891, eighty-five percent of Irishmen spoke English only and though fourteen percent spoke both English and Irish, only one percent of the total population relied on Irish as their sole means of communication. The Aran islands were among the few areas in the country to retain their native language in daily use throughout the course of the 19th century. The pressures to abandon the language were many. The business of the State, carried on in Aran by the police, the courts and the coastguards, was conducted only through English. Those who held salaried positions and lived a secure and comfortable lifestyle were all seen to be speakers of English. The National Education Acts of 1831 brought primary education to the islands in the second half of the century. The national schools ignored the language of the children's homes and did their best to create a generation of English speakers. Education brought the possibility of clerical and teaching jobs for some island children, jobs which demanded a knowledge of English rather than of Irish. Contact with the outside world increased decade by decade and English speaking scholars and tourists began to visit the islands to study the monasteries and duns. Most important of all, the majority of the young knew they would have to emigrate in search of a living. They would have to enter into, and seek to prosper in, an English speaking world in Britain or the United States. Though many emigrants preserved their language among their family and kin groups, in their new homes they had to equip themselves with the language of their workmates and neighbours. The Irish language was seen as a bar to successful emigration.

There was no awareness in the London-based Government or indeed among native Irish politicians that the preservation of the language was a matter of importance. The great political issues of Catholic Emancipation, Home Rule and the Land League were discussed and campaigned for through the English language. In 1891 the Congested Districts Board was set up in an effort to improve the economy of the poorer areas of the west. This Board certainly helped the islanders in their battle for survival but it too did not attach any importance to the preservation of the language.

All of these pressures were not without some result, even on Aran. The use of Irish declined on Inishmore, particularly in the vicinity of Kilronan where the forces in favour of English were most evident. Inisheer also suffered a decline, due in part to the presence there of a coastguard unit and to its nearness to the Co. Clare mainland where the language was rapidly losing ground. Only on the most isolated of the islands, Inishmaan did there remain a majority of people who were unable to speak English. Even here, the introduction of a national school resulted in some weakening of the position of Irish.

Isolation was a major factor in preserving the language on Aran. Even within the islands Irish fared best in those places which were furthest from the centres of administration and trade. But a review of the events of the 19th century in Ireland, and particularly in Aran, reveals an undeniable fact which is that a language cannot survive when the society which speaks that language is being destroyed and the people who learned it from the cradle are being forced to emigrate.

THE CONGESTED DISTRICTS BOARD

A century of hunger, disease, eviction and emigration finally aroused the conscience of the then Government, which set up the Congested Districts Board in 1891 in an attempt to improve social and economic conditions in the poorest parts of the country. A district was regarded as congested if the rateable valuation was less than 30/- (£1.50) per head of the population. The Congested Districts, then, were areas where each family did not have sufficient land to provide anything other than a very low standard of living. Almost all of the west coast, including the Aran Islands, was badly congested according to this definition.

The Congested Districts Board attempted to enlarge holdings where land could be bought or reclaimed. They encouraged domestic industries such as the knitting of sweaters and they sought to improve fishing by building piers and by providing nets and boats. There was no land available on Aran for redistribution but the Board met with some success in their efforts to encourage craftwork and fishing.

Before commencing work in each area the Board's inspectors made an inquiry into local conditions using a number of standard questions. These 'Base Line' reports are a reliable and accurate record of life in the Congested Districts. The report on the Aran Islands, which follows, gives a detailed picture of social and economic conditions on the islands at that time.

Confidential.

CONGESTED DISTRICTS BOARD FOR IRELAND.

COUNTY OF GALWAY—UNION OF GALWAY.

REPORT OF MAJOR RUTTLEDGE-FAIR, *Inspector.*

DISTRICT

OF

ARAN ISLANDS.

No. .

STATISTICAL TABLE.

ELECTORAL DIVISION.	Area in Statute Acres.	Poor Law Valuation.	Number of Ratings at and under £10 and above £4 Valuation.	Number of Ratings at and under £4 Valuation.	Population in 1891.	Number of Families in 1891.	Number of Families on Holdings exceeding £4 and under £2 Valuation.	Number of Families on Holdings at and under £2 Valuation.	Number of Families in very poor circumstances.	Number of Families which have no Cattle.
		£								
Inishmore,	11,288	1,576	117	578	2,907	562	186	279	60	30
TOTALS,	11,288	£1,576	117	578	2,907	562	186	279	60	30

(1.) Whether inland or maritime.

This district comprises a group of five inhabited islands at the entrance to Galway Bay; Inishmore or North Island, Inishmaan or Middle Island, Inisheer or South Island, and Straw and Rock Islands; the only people on the last two islands are lighthouse keepers and their families. Inishmore is by far the largest and most thickly populated, having nearly 2,000 inhabitants.

(2.) Average quantity of land cultivated on holdings at and under £4 valuation, under (a) oats, (b) potatoes, (c) meadow, (d) green crops.

There are on an average about one and three-quarter acres cultivated on holdings at and under £4 valuation, in the following way :—

Potatoes,	.	.	.	1¼ Acres.
Barley or Rye,	.	.	.	¼ ,,
Meadow,	.	.	.	¼ ,,

Total, 1¾ Acres.

A few perches of cabbages are also sown.

(3.) Extent of mountain or moor grazing, and rights possessed by tenants, whether in common or otherwise.

There is no mountain or moor grazing in this district.

(4.) Extent and description of land, if any, which could be profitably reclaimed and added to existing adjoining holdings.

There is no land in this district which could be profitably reclaimed and added to existing adjoining holdings.

(5.) Particulars as to any suitable land in the district which could be obtained, and to which families could be migrated with a reasonable prospect of success.

There is no suitable land in this district which could be obtained, and to which families could be migrated with a reasonable prospect of success.

No rotation of crops is followed in this district, the amount of land suitable for tillage being quite insufficient for such a purpose. Potatoes are the chief crop and are sown year after year in the same plots; about a rood of barley or rye, and in some instances, though rarely, oats is also sown. The soil being of a sandy nature is not suitable for growing oats. Sea-weed is the principal manure, thousands of tons of the best weed being washed ashore in stormy weather. As live stock are not housed during the winter months there is no farm-yard manure available.

The islanders possess a good breed of both cattle and sheep, the former being bred from good Shorthorn bulls imported from County Clare, and the latter crossed with rams bred in that County also. The Aran cattle always bring the highest price at the neighbouring fairs and markets on the mainland. The islanders are most anxious to secure a few well-bred Shorthorn bulls, and applications are about to be made to the Board for assistance. The usual fee charged for the bull's services is from 5s. to 7s., a much higher sum than is customary on the mainland. The islanders, however, do not object to such charges as it is well known bulls could not otherwise be profitably kept.

There are a number of fairly good mares on the North Island, but the sires are a very poor lot. A good Hackney stallion would, I think, be suitable to cross with the island mares, or better still, a Barb sire.

Pigs.—These are generally purchased on the mainland, sows not being kept.

Poultry—These are deteriorating; if a few sittings of eggs could be distributed through the islands, among reliable persons, an improvement might be easily effected.

Buyers from County Clare generally visit the islands in the spring and summer months to purchase live stock, and most of the cattle and sheep are sold to them. Any not disposed of in this way are taken to Galway and Spiddal fairs where they are eagerly sought after owing to their superior breed and fattening qualities. All supplies such as food, &c., are obtained at Galway. The number of eggs disposed of is insignificant as compared with other districts, though the people seem to have a number of fowls.

All communications are now carried on by steamer with Galway and a telegraph office has recently been opened at Kilronan.

The steamer only calls once a week at the Middle and South Islands.

There is scarcely any employment for labourers in this district; except in spring and summer. The rate of wage is 1s. 6d. per day and food.

There are no migratory labourers in this district.

It is said that more weaving, knitting, &c., was carried on formerly, as almost all the islanders, both young and old, then wore flannel; now the young people purchase considerable quantities of tweeds and other shop goods. Still flannel and frieze are a great deal worn, particularly by the Middle and South Islanders. Nothing woven or spun is ever sold, as far as I can learn.

More than two-thirds of the people burn kelp, and it is estimated that on an average each family makes at least two tons. The

average price is now quite £4 per ton, showing that nearly
£1,500 is paid for kelp in this district. Trade for the last two
years has been very brisk, and any quantity of good kelp can be
sold at very remunerative prices.

(14.) Sale of turf— nature
and extent of bogs

There is no turf on these islands.

(15.) Lobster fishing; number of men and boats em-
ployed.

Lobster fishing is not carried on to any appreciable extent by
the Aran islanders, though the Connemara fishermen catch
numbers of lobsters in the immediate vicinity.

(16.) Sea fishing—facilities
for sale of fish, and number of
men and boats solely employed
in fishing.

Sea fishing may be divided into three periods ; from December
to April for cod and ling ; from April to end of June, Spring
mackerel ; August to November, herring and Autumn mackerel.
Cod and ling fishing is carried on at present in small canvas-
covered canoes or curraghs manned by three men. These boats,
though very suitable in any reasonable weather for crossing from
island to island, are not safe for fishing purposes, especially
during the winter season, and much time is lost in enforced idle-
ness when the weather is at all unfavourable.
To develop this fishing, larger and better manned boats are
required.
The facilities for the sale of fish are now very good, especially
during the Spring mackerel fishing, but the people of the South
Island, who are nine miles from Kilronan, are very anxious that
the steamer should call twice instead of once a week, so as to
enable them to dispose of their fish more readily.

(17.) Number of boats and
men employed in fishing, or
carrying turf or sea-weed.
Classification of boats.

There are 116 curraghs, twelve small sailing boats, third class,
and four large trading boats in this district employed in fishing,
or carrying turf or sea-weed.

(18.) Fish ; whether con-
sumed at home or sold.

Cod and ling are sold to local buyers, who dispose of them in
Galway.

(19.) Extent of fish-curing.

Cod and ling are salted in a very rough way ; otherwise fish-
curing is unknown.

(20.) Piers and Harbours,
existing and suggested, and
how far those existing are
adapted to wants of district.

There are four piers on the islands—three on the North, Kilmurvey, Kilronan, and Killeany, and one on the Middle Island.
None of these piers are accessible at low water, and in other
respects, too, they are very faulty. The pier at Kilmurvey is
seriously damaged, and, unless repaired, will probably be swept
away by the next north-east storm. It is a useful structure, and
should not be allowed to remain in its present state. A comparatively small sum would repair the existing breach, and for
about £500 additional, an extension of about forty feet towards
deep water could be effected.
The pier at Kilronan is the most availed of, but it was wrongly
placed, and at low water is inaccessible even for small hookers.
It is evident if the Spring mackerel fishing continues to be
worked from Kilronan that a pier at which boats can come along-
side at any state of the tide for shelter, as well as for convenience,
should be provided. The bay is much exposed to north-east
gales, and should a storm spring up suddenly, as often occurs on
the West Coast, the fishing fleet would be placed in a very perilous
condition, under existing circumstances.
It has been proposed either to extend the present pier or build
a new one. So far as I can judge an extension of the present
pier would not effectively remedy the defects which now exist,
as there is no great depth of water south-west of the present
pier, and an extension therefore in that direction does not seem
sufficient to warrant the expenditure required. The alternative
scheme, viz., to build a new pier, is one which though involving
a large outlay, probably at least seven or eight thousand pounds,
would undoubtedly give the required facilities. The proposed
site is about 150 yards east of the existing pier and close to deep
water at all states of the tide.

The pier at Kilieany, though the most sheltered on the islands, is not accessible to large boats except at high water; I do not see how it could be improved.

On the Middle Island a pier built by the Board of Works is useful for landing turf, &c., &c., but it is too much exposed to allow boats to be kept there, neither can it be approached in bad weather.

I was shown a little cove on the south side of the Middle Island where the fishermen launch their curraghs from a rocky terrace which might be considerably improved by cutting away some projecting rocks and filling the cavities and fissures with concrete ; a pier could not be attempted, but a small expenditure would make the place much more accessible for curraghs.

(20.) Piers and Harbours, existing and suggested, and how far those existing are adapted to wants of district.

As regards the South Island, landing at any place in unsettled weather is both difficult and dangerous, and there is no place sufficiently sheltered that a pier which could be of any real use could be erected. A proposal has been put forward to make a harbour on this island by connecting Lough More with the sea. This lake covers an area of thirteen statute acres, and has a great depth of water, as much as ninety feet in places. It is situated at the east side of the island less than 300 yards from low water mark. The cutting through which boats would pass is not a long one, and if an entrance could once be made, boats of the largest size would be perfectly safe in any weather, and an invaluable harbour would be secured. The proposal is one worthy of very careful consideration, and in any event a survey should be made to determine the cost of the proposed works.

(21.) Extent of salmon and freshwater fisheries. Number of men earning their livelihood therefrom.

There are no salmon or freshwater fisheries in this district.

(22.) Banks and Loan Funds.

There are neither Banks nor Loan Funds in this district.

(23.) Mineral and other resources.

There are no mineral or other resources in this district.

(24.) Relative prevalence of cash or credit dealings, length of credit, interest charged, extent of barter, etc., etc.

Long credit is not now given; as a rule from three to six months to reliable customers is generally allowed. Shop-keepers' charge from twenty to twenty-five per cent. on all goods sold on credit. Considerable barter is carried on in fish, which are exchanged for sugar, flour, and tea, especially in the well-known village of Killeany.

(25.) Estimated *cash* receipts and expenditure of a family in ordinary circumstances.

The estimated *cash* receipts and expenditure of a family in ordinary circumstances, are as follow :—

RECEIPTS.	£	s.	d.	EXPENDITURE.	£	s.	d.
Sale of 5 pigs, .	10	0	0	Rent, .	3	0	0
„ cattle, .	7	0	0	Clerical dues, .	0	10	0
„ sheep, .	5	0	0	Clothes, .	6	0	0
„ 1 foal, .	5	0	0	Meal and flour, .	12	0	0
„ kelp, .	9	0	0	Groceries, .	6	11	0
„ eggs, .	1	0	0	Tobacco, .	2	12	0
„ butter, wool, and seaweed,	2	0	0	Spades, .	0	10	0
„ fish, .	3	0	0	Extras, .	2	0	0
				Turf, .	3	4	0
	£42	0	0		£36	7	0

The estimated *cash* receipts and expenditure of a family in poor circumstances are as follow :—

RECEIPTS.	£	s.	d.	EXPENDITURE.	£	s.	d.
Sale of 2 pigs, .	4	0	0	Rent, .	1	10	0
„ sheep, .	2	0	0	Clerical dues, .	0	5	0
„ fish, .	4	0	0	Clothes, .	5	0	0
„ 1 calf, .	4	0	0	Meal and flour, .	9	0	0
„ kelp, .	9	0	0	Groceries, .	3	10	0
„ seaweed, .	1	0	0	Tobacco, .	2	12	0
„ eggs, .	1	0	0	Turf, .	3	4	0
				Extras, .	1	0	0
	£25	0	0		£26	1	0

In good seasons potatoes generally last till the new crop is available, in the month of June. The value of home-grown food, consisting almost entirely of potatoes, may be estimated at from £12 to £15.

The dietary of the people of this district consists of potatoes, flour, tea, sugar, and fish. Three meals are taken daily ; one in the morning about nine o'clock, the second about one o'clock, and the evening meal between seven and eight o'clock. Meat is rarely used except on festive occasions, such as Christmas and Easter.

For my remarks upon the clothing of the people of this district, see paragraph 12 of this report.

The houses in this district are, as a rule, substantially built thatched cottages, containing three rooms, a kitchen, and two sleeping apartments, and except in the case of very poor people, they are fairly well furnished. In every respect, particularly as regards cleanliness, they are far superior to the houses occupied by the Connemara peasantry.

The people of the district are fairly industrious and hard-working, and may, I think, be depended upon to take advantage of any opportunity that may be afforded to improve their circumstances. Like most of the islanders on the West Coast they are very suspicious.

I am not aware of any organized effort having been made to develop the resources, or improve the condition of the people of this district.

It is evident that for islands so situated fishing should be the main resource of the people, yet owing to causes which the Board no doubt realise the islanders hitherto could not be considered fishermen. In only one village on the thickly populated North Island, and on the South Island, was fishing carried on to any appreciable extent.

The efforts recently made by the Board to provide a market and render the transit of fish comparatively easy have already borne fruit, and there is an eagerness now apparent amongst a considerable number of the people to apply themselves energetically to improving their condition by fishing. To thoroughly develop that industry at Aran it is most necessary that one or two places where boats can always be placed in safety and be able to proceed to sea in all weathers suitable for fishing should be provided, and I would therefore direct the attention of the Board to my suggestions in paragraph 20. The resources of the people might also be improved by the development of market gardening, an industry for which Aran, owing to the mildness of its climate during the winter and early spring months, is especially suitable.

Hitherto the difficulties of transport were an effectual barrier against any effort in this direction, but now the services of a steamer are available three times a week for the conveyance of produce to Galway where a market would soon be found. Further, the Arklow and other fishermen, who now make Aran their headquarters, are most anxious to purchase vegetables if they could be obtained, and have constantly told me they would be willing to give the highest price for them.

I think premiums for the best plots of early potatoes, white turnips, cabbages, &c., &c., should be offered by the Board, and if this course was adopted the industry would probably get a fair start.

Early in February I saw at the Aran Coast-guard Station potatoes over ground, which had been sown shortly before Christmas.

31st March, 1893.

ROBERT RUTTLEDGE-FAIR,
Inspector.

Dún Eochla dominates the Eastern end of Inishmore from its hill top position. Nearby are the remains of the lighthouse built in the early 19th century but later abandoned. The limestone pavement in the foreground, strewn with loose rocks and criss-crossed by fissures, is devoid of vegetation.

place names of aran

All these places are marked on the map, pages 8 and 9

INISHMORE / INIS MÓR
(The Big Island)

Arkyne's Castle
A castle built near Killeany by the O'Briens. Later it was rebuilt by Cromwellian soldiers, using stones from St. Enda's monastery.

Baile na m'Bocht
The remains of a stone wall found here may once have been part of the walls of a dun.

Brannock Island / Oileán dá Bhranóg
The Irish means "the island of the two little ravens". It is situated west of Inishmore.

Bun Gowla / Bun Gabhla
"The bottom of the fork" – it is the westernmost village on the island.

Cowrugh / Corrúch
A village on the road between Kilronan and Kilmurvey.

Dún Aengus / Dún Aonghasa
"Aengus Fort" – it is said that Aengus was one of the chiefs of the Fir Bolg. Dún Aengus is built on the edge of a high cliff overlooking the Atlantic.

Dún Dúchathair
"The Black Fort" Cathair is another name for a stone fort. Dún Dúchathair is a promontory fort, on the south west of the island.

Dún Eochla
"The Fort of the Yew Wood". Dún Eochla is built near the highest point on Inishmore. Its site was later chosen for the building of a lighthouse.

Dún Eonaghta
"The Fort of the Eonaght Family". They are said to have been a Munster clan who once ruled Aran. Dún Eonaghta is built on good land.

Glassan Rock
The south eastern point of the island, from which fishing for 'wrasse' takes place.

Gort na gCapall
"The Field of the Horses". This is the only village on the western seaboard of the island. Liam O'Flaherty the author was born here.

Iarairne
Possible means "The Back of the Island". Locally it is known as The Dog's Head because of its shape.

Killeany / Cill Éinne
The Irish means St. Enda's Church. St. Enda built his monastery here. It is the second largest village on the island and once was quite a busy fishing port.

Kilmurvey / Cill Mhuirbhigh
The Irish means "the Church near the sandy beach". Quite a good road runs from Kilronan to the village of Kilmurvey.

Kilronan / Cill Rónáin
The Irish means St. Ronan's Church. It is the largest village on the Aran Islands. Its harbour, built with the help of the Congested District s Board, is large enough for the steamer from Galway. Most of the goods – foodstuffs, building materials, fuel etc. – imported to the islands are delivered to Kilronan, and then collected by their owners.

Loch Port Charrugh
A lagoon cut off from the sea, on the north of the island.

Mainistir
A village west of Kilronan.

Oghil / Eochaill
Eochaill is a townland not far from Kilronan.

Onaght / Eoghanacht
A townland near the site of the Seven Churches Monastery. Birthplace of M. O'Direain.

Poll na bPéist
"The Serpent's Hole". This is one of the most spectacular puffing holes on the island.

Poll na Brioscharnach
A sea arch on the south of the island.

Poll na gCapall
A turloch (an impermanent lake) located east of Kilmurvey.

Port Murvey / Port Mhuirbhigh
A village situated at the narrow neck of the island.

Rock Island / An t'Oileán Iarthach

An island west of Inishmore. A lighthouse was erected here in the mid-nineteenth century.

Sruthan
Located between Kilmurvey and Onaght where an intermittent stream is found.

Straw Island / Oileán na Tuí
A small island off the south-east coast of Inishmore. In times past rye was grown here for thatching.

Teaghlach Éinne
"St. Enda's House". One of the only buildings remaining from St. Enda's monastery.

Teampall a'Phoill
"The Church in the Hollow" – this is one of the ruins of the Seven Churches monastery near Onaght.

Teampall Asurnai
Situated west of Kilronan and perhaps dedicated to the female saint Soarney.

Teampall Bheanáin
"St. Benan's Church", another remaining building of St. Enda's monastery.

Teampall Breacháin

"St. Brecan's Church". This is the largest ruin on the site of the Seven Churches monastery. St. Brecan, one of St. Enda's disciples founded this monastery. He is very highly honoured by the people of Aran.

Teampall na Ceathrar Álainn

"The Church of the Four Beautiful Ones". The 'beautiful ones' were said to be four saints called Fursey, Brendan of Birr, Conall and Berchan. It is located near the village of Cowrugh.

Teampall Chiaráin

"St. Kieran's Church" is situated near Mainistir, a village west of Kilronan. St. Kieran is said to be the same saint who founded the great monastery at Clonmacnoise on the River Shannon in AD 545.

Teampall MacDuach

This church is dedicated to St. Colman, patron saint of sailors. It is situated near Kilmurvey.

Teampall na Naomh

"The Church of the Saints" near Kilmurvey.

An Trá Mór

"The Big Strand", a large sandy beach on the south-east end of the island.

An Turloch Mór

A turloch (an impermanent lake) located between Killeany and Kilronan.

INISHMAAN / INIS MEÁIN
(The Middle Island)

Dún Conor / Dún Chonchúir

"Conor's Fort". It is not known who Conor was. Dun Conor is a magnificent ring-fort on a hill overlooking Inishmaan.

Dún Moher

Also called Dún Fhearbhaigh (Farvey's Fort).

Kilcanaragh / Cill Cheannach

"St. Kenanagh's Church". Some say that Kenanagh is another name for St. Gregory. Gregory's Sound between Inishmore and Inishmaan is said to be named after him.

Teampall na Seacht Mac Ri

"The Church of the Seven Princes". It is not known to whom this church is dedicated.

INISHEER / INIS ÓIRR
(The Eastern Island)

Cill na Seacht n'Iníon

"The Church of the Seven Daughters". It is not known who the daughters in question were.

Dún Formna

"The Fort of the Ridge". This is the only remaining fort on Inisheer. Within its walls stand the ruins of O'Brien Castle.

Teampall Chaomháin

"St. Cavan's Church" – according to legend, St. Cavan was the brother of St. Kevin of Glendalough, Co. Wicklow. The islanders pray to St. Cavan in times of illness.

Teampall Ghobnait

"St. Gobnet's Church". St. Gobnet was one of Ireland's best loved women saints. and is said to have spent some time on Inisheer. She is the patron saint of beekeepers, and is still honoured on the islands, even though nobody keeps bees there. She and St. Soarney on Inishmore are the only women saints associated with Aran.

ACKNOWLEDGEMENTS

We would like to thank Ann Jackson and Brian Kavanagh for work in the development of the materials; Tim O'Neill for reading and commenting on the manuscript; Mr. Seamus Heaney for 'The Evening Land', 'Inisheer' and 'The Oarsman's Song'; A. D. Peters and Co. Ltd. for extracts from *Famine* by Liam O'Flaherty.

In instances where we have failed to trace the copyright holder, we would be grateful if they would contact the publisher.

We would like to thank the following for permission to reproduce photographs: Pat Langan and *The Irish Time* 76, 80; Bord Failte Eireann, 18 t the National Museum of Ireland 24